COPYRIGHT

Owen Janssen

THANK YOU GIFT

As a thank you gift to my readers, I have a little surprise I hope you will enjoy...

A FREE Copy of one of our newest and most exciting books! *"WORLD WONDERS: A Captivating Compilation Of Random Trivia, Fascinating Facts, And Curious Tidbits To Catch The Quick-Witted Off Guard"*

YOUR FREE BOOK – Upcoming Code!

"WORLD WONDERS: A Captivating Compilation Of Random Trivia, Fascinating Facts, And Curious Tidbits To Catch The Quick-Witted Off Guard"

WORLD WONDERS

To obtain your **FREE** copy of ***WORLD WONDERS***
- Scan The Code Below, Or Simply Head to:

https://bit.ly/WORLDWONDERSFREE

READ OUR NEWEST BOOKS AT NO COST BEFORE THEY HIT THE SHELVES

Are you an avid reader who loves being the first to discover the latest bestsellers? Joining Advanced Reader Copy (ARC) teams gives you the exclusive opportunity to read books before they hit the shelves! Not only do you get to enjoy the excitement of being among the first to read new releases, but you also have the chance to provide valuable feedback to authors and publishers, helping to shape the final version of the book. The best part is, you'll receive each and every single one for *free*. So, if you want to be at the forefront of the literary world and have a say in the next big thing, sign up to our ARC team today!

UPCOMING ARC

Scan the upcoming code for details. Or, simply head to https://owenjanssenarc.com/

CONTACT ME

If you enjoy reading this book, I would be so appreciative if you took the time to leave a review.

It means the world *to authors such as myself.* Or, if you would like to chat with me directly, I would love to hear from you! Contact me at **support@owenjanssen.com** or head to **owenjanssen.com**.

EPIC TRUE TALES AND CRAZY STORIES

A genuinely hilarious book of outrageous events, entertaining world history, and funny true stories for adults! With humorous questions and answers throughout

Owen Janssen

CONTENTS

Introduction

Truth is stranger than fiction, as the old saying goes. The truth can also be far more entertaining than fiction because life gets really bizarre sometimes.

In *EPIC TRUE TALES AND CRAZY STORIES,* you'll find a collection of stories that will amaze and entertain you. The book includes interesting events from history, fascinating tales about the animal kingdom, the biggest hoaxes of all time, some really dumb crime stories, and more. Oh, and don't forget the interesting facts about several celebrities.

All the tales are told with a healthy dollop of humor and wry wisdom. You'll have a hard time putting the book down before the last page is read.

Join me now for a look at the stories that have made the world a more interesting place but were never taught in history class.

Chapter 1: History's Hidden Side

History books are filled with fascinating stories, telling tales of brave soldiers and daring adventurers. Those stories, however, only show parts of the full picture.

Even politicians, who we might think of as dull and dour, can sometimes be odd fellows. There's no shortage of weird happenings involving political figures that occurred over the years.

Join me in this chapter to explore some lesser known facts, as well as a couple of events that were so strange that we rather forgot about them—until now.

The World's Shortest War

Wars usually rage on for decades. They can engulf the entire world, changing the course of history and bringing misery to millions of people.

However, one war did things completely differently and even made it into the Guinness Book of World Records as the shortest war in history.

The year was 1896 and the scene was the East African island of Zanzibar, which was a British colony at the time. A new sultan came to power after the death of the previous one, without the approval of the English overlords. The British Empire wanted someone else as ruler in Zanzibar, but Khalid bin Barghash was having none of that and moved into the royal palace. Warnings about dire consequences from the British government didn't faze the new sultan and he stuck to his position.

The Brits were not happy being defied and promptly sent warships to bombard the palace. The brave, new sultan only needed 38 minutes of battle before he decided on a political change of heart and fled the palace.

A Sticky End

A strange, but unfortunately not sweet, story from Boston, U.S. took place in 1919. The town housed a huge molasses tank belonging to a distilling company that provided industrial alcohol, made from fermented molasses, for the war effort.

Alcohol was an important ingredient in the production of weapons and ammunition.

Molasses is a thick, sticky, and intensely sweet substance obtained when sugar cane is refined. The tank on Boston's waterfront was immense at more than 50 feet high and 90 feet in diameter. It could hold up to 2.5 million gallons of the precious molasses.

Construction of the tank was finished as quickly as possible to get the alcohol into production, but that led to the tank leaking and strange rumblings coming from it, right from the start.

After the war, the distillery continued using the tank to produce grain alcohol. Prohibition was nearing its end in the U.S. and grain alcohol was in high demand, causing the tank to be used to full capacity, 24/7.

During the afternoon of January 15, 1919, the overstressed tank burst. Eyewitnesses later reported that the huge wave of molasses that hit the town reached as high as 40 feet in some places.

The thick syrup hardened quickly in the cold weather and, besides extensive damage to infrastructure, 21 people also unfortunately lost their lives. Boston reportedly still smelled of molasses years later.

The War Australia Lost to Birds

Australians are well-known for their pluck, especially where facing wild animals are concerned. The country's famous flightless birds, the emus, however once proved more than the Aussies could face.

After WWI, many ex-soldiers returned to their home countries with nowhere to go and no jobs to do. The economic woes were exacerbated by the global Great Depression.

The Australian government tackled the problem by launching a farming program specifically for war veterans. They were given land in the western region of the country where they proceeded to plant crops.

By November 1932, the whole project faced serious obstacles when several of the farmers threatened to leave. About 20,000 emus had migrated further inland when their breeding season started, and they were eating the crops.

The government called on the ex-soldiers to help them get rid of the scourge. Armed with machine guns, the farmer-soldiers started a war on the emus.

After about 38 days, however, the soldiers had to admit they had underestimated the cunning of the birds. The feathered fighters quickly learned to split up into numerous small groups that were simply too fast and keen-eyed for the humans.

The Great Emu War, as it has since become known, thus ended with full marks to the ornithological side.

A Roman Lesson in Self-Worth

Roman emperor Julius Caesar is not known in history for being particularly humble. His high esteem of his self-worth started at a young age already, as a band of pirates in the Aegean Sea found out.

As a 25-year-old nobleman in 75 B.C.E., Julius set out by boat from his home in Italy to study oratory in Rhodes, one of the Greek islands. A merry band of pirates attacked his boat, taking him captive and setting a ransom for his freedom at 20 talents. Laughing in their faces, Caesar berated them for not knowing who they captured and suggested a more fitting ransom of 50 talents.

That was only the beginning of the pirates' encounter with the strangest captive they ever had. He settled in among them but bossed them around as if their roles were reversed. When he took part in their games, he addressed them like subordinates and refused to take any orders from them. He even threatened to have them all crucified—something they treated as a joke from their nutty captive.

The ransom was delivered after 38 days, and Caesar went free. He managed to gather an army in the Turkish city of Miletus, despite holding no military or public office, and set out to round the pirates up.

When the governor of Asia seemed unsure how to punish them, Caesar made good on his promise by going to the prison himself and having them all crucified.

A City of Coincidence

In 1913, Vienna was a place where many interesting political, intellectual, and artistic characters found themselves. At the time, the city was the capital of the Austro-Hungarian Empire—a sprawling region comprising 15 nations and more than 50 million inhabitants.

There was no strict, totalitarian government; something that created a haven for political dissidents, especially from other countries. Two men from this category, who met each other for the first time in Vienna before they started shaping the world for most of the 20th century, were Joseph Stalin and Leon Trotsky.

Trotsky was a Russian intellectual who was living in near-exile in Vienna when Stalin arrived there in January 1913. His radically Marxist newspaper, "Pravda," put him in direct opposition to the official Russian political sentiments at the time.

Iosif Vissarionovich Dzhugashvili, now remembered in history as Joseph Stalin, was a Russian political activist who visited Vienna on Lenin's orders. He was to make contact with Austrian revolutionary thinkers.

Trotsky and Stalin initially found much common ground but became political enemies in the 1920s.

Just a few miles from where Trotsky and Stalin had their first meeting, one of Vienna's most famous coffeehouses, Cafe Landtmann, regularly hosted the psychologist known as the father of psychoanalysis, Sigmund Freud. The city had (and still has) a culture of spending time in coffeehouses to meet new people and, above all, to debate and talk.

Trotsky and another man that became notorious some years later as German leader, Adolf Hitler, favored Cafe Central that was just a few minutes' walk from Freud's haunt.

Just south of Vienna, in Wiener Neustadt, a young man by the name of Josip Broz worked in the Daimler factory. Broz later became Yugoslavia's leader Marshal Tito.

It is not known whether all five of them ran into each other at some point, but it's certainly possible. Playwrights Laurence Marks and Maurice Gran have certainly imagined what it might have been like; their 2007 radio play "Dr. Freud will see you now, Mr. Hitler" explored the "What if?" question.

Fly Me To the Moon In the 17th Century

Bishop Dr. John Wilkins firmly believed that travel to the moon was possible. What makes this astonishing, however, is the fact that the bishop lived in the 1600s.

The 17th century was an exciting time; microscopes became powerful enough to reveal the details of individual cells, Galileo was making stunning astronomical discoveries with the help of the telescope, and people became more inclined to look for empirical evidence instead of just accepting superstitions. It is understandable that Bishop Wilkins believed anything was possible.

The clergyman was also convinced that he knew exactly how humans were going to get to the moon. He wrote a book in 1638 in which he set out his theories to prove the moon was a habitable world, and that man could easily go there.

He proposed using an open chariot with a vertical, rotating sail protruding from the back to lift a couple of men high enough to escape the pull of the earth. Gravity was, in those days, understood to be something like a magnet that could be left behind if you could get high enough up from the ground.

He sealed his theory with the firm conviction that the Creator of all things would never have made a world like the moon without someone to inhabit it.

He reportedly experimented with several mechanical contraptions in the garden of Wadham College at Oxford, where he worked as the Warden. As no positive results were ever noted, one has to assume that his theories did not take off.

A Unique Prescription

The English statesman Winston Churchill loved his tipple. Having to go without it during an upcoming 40-stop lecture tour in America terrified him, but he was going to try; the year was 1931 and prohibition was strictly in force throughout the U.S.

Shortly after arriving in New York in December 1931, Churchill rushed to an appointment with the financier Bernard Baruch. Getting impatient with the slow progress of his cab, he jumped out to cross the street on foot.

Forgetting to look both ways, he was struck down by a car approaching from his right at about 35 mph. Another cab took him to the hospital where he was admitted with a sprained shoulder, fractured ribs, a fractured nose, and a deep gash to the head.

The canceled lectures put his finances under strain and after six weeks, he forced himself to undertake a shortened, 14-week tour.

Churchill was still in a considerable amount of pain and appealed to the physician who admitted him to hospital for some help. Dr.

Otto Pickhardt then wrote him a prescription known as a "Get Out of Prohibition Free Pass."

According to the note, Churchill was to be allowed the consumption of unlimited amounts of alcohol to aid in his recovery. The good doctor also stipulated that a daily minimum of 250 cubic centimeters had to be maintained, which adds up to about four standard doubles.

The King Who Ate Himself to Death

The Swedish king Adolf Frederick ruled the country between 1751 and 1771. His reign formed part of the time in Swedish history that is known as The Age of Liberty.

King Adolf granted much freedom to the press, extended civil rights, and steered the country through a long time of peace.

Unfortunately, today, he is better remembered for the manner of his death.

To say the king loved food is somewhat of an understatement. He had an unusually large appetite and regularly indulged in huge meals.

The Swedish Christians had a custom of gorging themselves on foods they would not be allowed to eat during Lent. The feasting happened on what they called Shrove Tuesday. Lent started on a Wednesday and lasted for the next 40 days, commemorating the fasting period Jesus observed in the desert.

King Adolf wholeheartedly endorsed this custom, and on Shrove Tuesday in 1771 he sat down to an overly large meal of pleasurable foods.

Besides the caviar, lobsters, kippers, boiled meats, and sauerkraut he washed down with champagne, he ended his meal with a pastry-type dessert called semla.

Semlas are buns made from white flour and filled with cream. They were served to the king in bowls of hot milk, flavored with cinnamon and raisins.

After wolfing down 14 semlas, Adolf at last decided to stop eating. Later that same day, he developed severe digestive problems and eventually died from indigestion.

The Day Richard Nixon Became a Drug Mule

Besides the 1972 Watergate spy scandal, American ex-president Richard Nixon was also known as a staunch opponent of drug use. He started campaigning against it when he was still vice-president.

During the cold war with the Soviet Union in the 1950s, the American government started sending some of their best African-American artists, musicians, writers, and athletes on tours through Asia and Europe as goodwill ambassadors. The hugely successful jazz musician Louis Armstrong, also known as Satchmo, got his turn late in the 1950s.

Satchmo loved smoking marijuana and had been in trouble with the law a couple of times before arriving back on American soil after his third goodwill tour. He was, therefore, understandably stressed when he was unexpectedly asked to join the queue for customs; he was carrying three pounds of marijuana in his luggage.

While waiting in line and sweating profusely, vice-president Nixon entered the room, followed by reporters and photographers. Spotting Satchmo, Nixon asked him what he was doing standing in that queue. When he explained that airport staff directed him to customs, Nixon said ambassadors did not need to go through customs. He offered to take the musician's bags through customs himself—an offer that was gratefully accepted.

Without knowing it, Nixon thereby smuggled prohibited drugs into the country.

When told about it years later, Nixon's only dismay was about the fact that Satchmo really smoked weed.

World Peace and Hangovers All Round

When WWII ended, the Russians were so elated that they partied themselves clean out of vodka.

The news that Germany was finally defeated broke on Radio Moscow at 10 minutes past one on the morning of May 9, 1945. Being the true vodka lovers they are, Russia's citizens grabbed a drink or five, ran into the streets in their pajamas, and started celebrating.

Only 22 hours later, there wasn't a drop of their favorite tipple left in the whole country. Even though vodka production had carried on without interruption (and was even expanded) throughout the war to generate revenue for the national defense budget, the relieved and happy Russians finished it all.

The nationwide hangover resulting from the party was the least of their worries. Vodka production was the government's main source of income and having nothing to sell or export put them in a unique kind of crisis. They did, however, waste no time to pick up their production again.

The Price of Poor Practice

Musicians and other entertainers were very important in the Middle Ages and people took their skills seriously. Anyone found wanting in the performance department could find themselves facing harsh consequences.

One of the punishments meted out to entertainers who skipped a few practice sessions was wearing what was known as the "shame flute."

The so-called flute was a tube similar in form to the modern clarinet, but made of heavy iron, and with an iron loop at the narrow end. The loop was forced over the entertainer's head and his hands were bound around the tube, held by more iron loops.

He was then paraded through the streets, "playing the shame flute," and everyone knew he brought disgrace to his art. Besides the insults and jeers, the wearer of the shame flute also had rotten eggs and tomatoes thrown at him.

The 49-Year Whisky War

A good natured "war," in which whisky was the mark of the "aggressor," continued for 49 years in the Arctic. The issue was only amicably resolved in June 2022.

The story started in 1973, when a treaty was signed to demarcate the maritime border between Denmark and Canada. The border line goes through a tiny island that lies halfway between the two countries.

Ownership of the tiny piece of land, known as Hans Island, was claimed by both countries. Canada argued the island formed part of territory transferred to them in 1880 by the Hudson Bay Company, while Denmark regarded it as part of Greenland.

Both countries sent troops to Hans Island occasionally. The soldiers used to raise the particular country's flag, before leaving a bottle of the finest whisky that country had to offer, next to the flagpole.

The whole "war" always remained friendly, even leading to some good-natured sparring at times in the parliaments of both countries. In 2011, a member of the opposition in Canada suggested light-heartedly that an ambassador be sent to Hans Island as a means of exile, to which the minister of foreign affairs replied that he would not allow the opposition to give away an island and undermine Canada's sovereignty.

An agreement concluded on June 14, 2022, finally ended the matter. The two countries agreed to a division of the island along a natural ridge. About 60% of Hans Island went to Denmark and the rest to Canada.

The agreement established both the longest maritime border anywhere, and the first land border between Canada and Denmark.

A Motorcycle Mystery

Imagine having a totally unique motorcycle, and then having to hide it inside a bricked-up wall.

That is what happened to a one-of-a-kind 1916 Traub bike in Chicago in the U.S. A plumber was called to a house in 1967 to fix a leak. To get to the trouble spot, he had to tear down a wall. Great was his surprise when he saw an old motorcycle, in top condition, hidden behind the bricks.

The current home owner had no idea the bike was there. When the former owner was contacted, he explained that his son stole the Traub all those years ago. When his father found out about it, he was so angry that he forced his son to enlist in the army. The young man secretly bricked up the beautiful motorcycle with the idea to take it out when he returned from military duty.

Unfortunately, the son was sent to fight in WWI, and he perished in the fighting. The motorcycle remained hidden for 50 years.

Motorcycle experts have been astonished by the bike's originality and unique design ever since it was discovered. There is no similar model in the history of American motorcycles.

The bike was traced to Gottlieb Richard Traub, a motorcycle repairman who also described himself as an experimental machinist on his draft card for the war.

The mystery only deepened when it was discovered that the unique motorcycle was never reported stolen by Traub.

The real story died with Traub in 1952 and will probably never be known.

A Basket Case

Getting home after having a bit too much to drink at a pub can be a problem, especially in countries where you can't just call a cab.

Pub owners in Istanbul, Turkey, implemented an ingenious solution in the 1960s. They employed casual laborers at night known as "basket men" ("küfeci" in Turkish). Their only job was to carry drunk patrons home in baskets on their backs.

The Turkish word for being too drunk to walk is "küfe." That gave rise to a local expression still used today, "küfelik olmak," meaning being so intoxicated that the only way you'll get home is by being carried home in a basket.

Hoarding... and Then Some

Junk has a sneaky way of piling up; one day the house is under control, and the next, you're thinking about a thorough spring clean.

Two New York brothers found this out the hard way and became legendary hoarders in the 1930s. Homer and Langley Collyer lived with their mother (after their parents' divorce) at 2078 Fifth Avenue, Harlem until her death in 1929. Having never married or lived on their own, the brothers stayed on together in the brownstone.

Homer had studied maritime law earlier, while his brother qualified in chemistry and engineering. After their mother died, Homer continued his law practice; Langley traded in pianos.

In 1932, Homer suffered a stroke that left him blind. Langley quit his job to look after his brother and their lives, which had always been somewhat eccentric, started derailing completely.

They fully withdrew from society and lived on a diet of oranges, black bread, and peanut butter. Their utilities had been shut down for failure to pay, so Langley jerry-rigged an old car engine to use as a generator.

When the rheumatism Homer had also developed left him completely paralyzed, Langley's mental state started deteriorating. He never left the house before midnight to forage for food, returning also with heaps of junk.

The rusted bikes, empty bottles, broken baby carriages and much, much more piled up to the extent that the doors of the house could not be opened anymore, and it was impossible to move around inside. Langley built a "nest" for each of them and fashioned tunnels through the junk to move through. He booby-trapped the tunnels to deter any would-be burglars.

Eventually, on March 21, 1947, New York police received an anonymous call about a stench coming from 2078 Fifth Avenue. After breaking into the house and digging through the junk for five hours, they found Homer's body. He'd been dead for 10 hours from starvation and heart failure.

Langley's body was, however, nowhere to be found. Authorities started cleaning up the mess and removed more than 120 tons of hoarded rubbish. Three weeks later, one of the workmen found Langley lying dead in one of the tunnels. It seems like one of his own booby-traps tripped him, bringing piles of rusted bed springs, tin cans, old newspapers, and hundreds of books down on him.

The official verdict was that he had died weeks earlier. That left Homer without anyone to care for him, which caused his death from starvation.

Coincidence, or Comet Curse?

Mark Twain is a celebrated American author, humorist, and lecturer who was born in 1835 as Samuel Langhorne Clemens. His best-known books about the adventures of Tom Sawyer and Huckleberry Finn are still favorites of kids all over, to this day.

Clemens' birth took place two weeks after Halley's comet reached its closest point to the sun in its elliptical orbit, making it visible from Earth.

The comet appears every 75 to 76 years and was due to show itself again in 1910. Twain himself said in 1909 that he expected to "go out with the comet" because he had appeared with it.

True to his prediction, he died on April 21, 1910. That was the day after the comet had again reached its perihelion, being closest to the sun.

Solving the Mystery of the "Mary Celeste"

The story of the ghost ship "Mary Celeste" that was found intact, but completely deserted, on December 5, 1872, is well-known. The captain of the ship, Benjamin Briggs, started out with a cargo of alcohol from New York for Italy the previous month, but never arrived there. The ship was found about 400 nautical miles (460 miles) from Portugal.

The lifeboat was gone, the cargo hatch was open, and there was a strong rope trailing from the back of the ship into the sea, but there were no signs of life or of any struggle.

Several years later, investigators hit upon the fact that nine of the 1,700 oak barrels in the cargo hold were empty, while all the others were still full. The empty barrels were made of red oak and the rest were created out of white oak. Red oak is porous, but white oak is watertight.

The investigation concluded that 300 gallons of alcohol evaporated into the hold from the red oak barrels, creating an explosion hazard. The crew opened the hatch to get rid of the fumes, but it did not work.

The safest solution they could devise was to get into the lifeboat, tying it to the ship with a strong rope. The idea was to trail behind the ship at a safe distance.

Unfortunately, the rope seems to have been accidentally severed before they could figure out how to deal with the alcohol, and the captain, his family, and his crew were left adrift in the Atlantic Ocean.

A Cursed Opera

The headline is not the lament of someone who hates opera; Richard Wagner's opera "Tristan und Isolde" is widely documented as being cursed from the day the composer started writing it.

Wagner was penniless and on the run from authorities when he started working on his new opera in 1857, living alone in Switzerland. After about a year, his wife Minna, whom he had left behind in Germany, discovered his affair with the wife of his chief supporter at the time. Minna eventually left her husband but never legally divorced him.

The music Wagner wrote for the opera is notoriously difficult for both the male and female leads and it took him five years to finish it. He then struggled for another six years to find an opera house and soloists prepared to premiere it.

Wagner eventually persuaded Ludwig and Malvina Schnorr von Carolsfeld, two of the greatest opera stars of the time, to take the lead parts. The leading conductor of the time, Hans von Bülow, held the baton.

After 70 grueling rehearsals, "Tristan und Isolde" opened on June 10, 1865, at the Bavarian State Opera. The opening night had been scheduled for May 15, but Malvina's voice suddenly and dramatically disappeared, and they had to wait for her to get well again.

The public and critics gave the opera a disastrous reception, but Wagner was not fazed. He continued with the performances until the sudden death of Ludwig Schnorr von Carolsfeld on July 21, 1865, at the age of 29. The cause of his death is unknown.

His wife Malvina ended her career shortly afterward.

The event that finally clinched the idea of a curse for believers were the deaths of two conductors of the opera while conducting their respective performances, 57 years apart.

Felix Mottl died in 1911 in Münich while conducting the 100th performance of the opera. Wagner expert Joseph Keilberth met his untimely death in 1968 while standing on the same spot and in front of the same orchestra where Mottl died.

Mongolia's Wrestling Warrior Princess

Princess Khutulun was born in 1260 as the daughter of a khan and the great-great-granddaughter of Genghis Khan. She grew up as the only girl among her 14 brothers.

From an early age, Khutulun excelled at physical activities such as archery, horse riding, and sumo wrestling. She became a fearsome warrior, fighting alongside her beloved father against the forces of her cousin, Kublai Khan, who wanted to force Mongolians to adopt the Chinese way of living.

The warrior princess refused to marry a man who could not beat her in a wrestling match. The potential suitors had to wager horses before the bout started.

It is said that Khutulun defeated 1,000 men and accumulated 10,000 horses before eventually marrying someone of her choice.

The Surgeon With a 300% Mortality Rate

The 1800s were difficult for patients. Operations had to be performed without anesthetic as we know it, because it had not been developed yet. Speed was of the essence to minimize pain and stress for the patients and increase their chances for survival.

British doctor, Robert Liston, was known as the fastest surgeon alive. He was also quite the showman and frequently told onlookers to time him during an operation.

One day during a leg amputation, he moved so fast that he cut off two of his assistant's fingers. While switching knives, he accidentally slashed against the coat of an elderly doctor who was looking on.

The old gentleman thought he was cut and collapsed with a heart attack from the shock. A few days later, both the patient and the assistant died from gangrene that was probably caused by dirt from the saw in their wounds.

Games for the Afterlife

The ancient Egyptians loved their board games so much that the Pharaohs even had games buried with them in their elaborate tombs.

Four of the most popular games were Twenty Squares, Hounds and Jackals, Senet, and Mehen. Senet is the best-known, with many scenes of people, from royalty to ordinary citizens, playing the game depicted on walls and in tombs. King Tutankhamun loved Senet so much that he was buried with five game boxes.

The Egyptian word "senet" means "passing." It didn't take long for the game to become associated with traveling to the afterlife after death. Some of the squares on the board represent the challenges a person might have to overcome in his journey, while others depict some help to negotiate the hazards.

The Glass Delusion

Between the 15th and 17th centuries, many wealthy people in Europe became afflicted with a psychiatric disorder known as the glass delusion. They became convinced that their bodies were made of glass and could shatter after the slightest touch.

The first case recorded in history was King Charles VI of France. He had all his clothing reinforced with iron rods and did not allow any of his advisors to come near him.

Famous 19th century Russian composer Peter Ilyich Tchaikovsky might also have been suffering from the glass delusion. He believed his head would fall off while he was conducting an orchestra if he did not hold it.

Modern scholars linked the disorder to melancholy and depression. The emergence of glass during that time as an item exclusively for the rich and noble might also have strengthened the delusion.

The Cadaver Synod

A ninth century pope, Stephen VI, put the corpse of his predecessor on trial in 897.

Popes crowned the Holy Roman Emperor in those days, and they could not escape political intrigue. Pope Formosus, who had died nine months earlier, had crowned King Arnulf of the East Franks as one of his last tasks. The crowning was still in dispute when Stephen took over in the Vatican.

Stephen favored someone else and, in order to get Formosus' rulings nullified, put him on trial.

Attendants had to clothe the corpse in his ecclesiastical robes and prop the body up on the papal throne. Stephen appointed a deacon to speak on behalf of Formosus.

After convicting Formosus of usurping the papacy, his decrees were reversed, the three fingers with which he had given blessings in life were cut off, and his body was thrown into the Tiber River.

Stephen's reign did not last long, however. He was arrested and killed in jail just over a year after coming to power.

When Christmas Was Banned by Christians

It sounds unlikely, but the conservative Christians of the 1600s, who were known as Puritans, banned Christmas celebrations in 1659.

To understand why, it is necessary to consider how Christmas was celebrated at the time.

Christmas comes from a pagan tradition celebrating the winter solstice. It was a rowdy festival with plenty of drinking and misbehaving. Poor people would go to their wealthy neighbors demanding treats. If they were refused, things often got violent.

Puritanism rejected any excesses, and anyone caught celebrating Christmas was fined five shillings.

The ban was lifted in 1681, but only because they were pressured to bring the colony's laws in line with English laws.

Death by Tortoise

The man who is known as the father of the Greek tragedy, Aeschylus, is the only person in history whose death can be attributed directly to a tortoise.

In 456, Aeschylus returned to Sicily. While he was out walking, an eagle picked up a tortoise to eat. Mistaking the playwright's bald head for a rock, he dropped the tortoise on Aeschylus' head and killed him.

A President With a Beer Philosophy

Abe Lincoln was not only America's 16th president, taking office in 1861, but he is also famous for his quote about politics and beer: "I am a firm believer in the people. If given the truth, they can be depended upon to meet any national crisis. The great point is to bring them the real facts, and beer."

Although Lincoln himself seems, from various historical sources, to have been either a teetotaler or a very light drinker, he realized the value of alcohol for some people.

He was born into a family who worked in the liquor industry and later opened a grocery store where liquor could be purchased as well. He always denied criticism about helping to fuel misconduct, saying that no patrons were allowed to consume the alcohol they bought on the premises.

On July 1, 1862, Lincoln signed amendments to the American tax law that made it legal to levy excise duties on several items, including beer. The money collected was used to fund the civil war effort against the southern states.

Bonus Interrogation

1. How long was the world's shortest war?

2. Which big names lived in Vienna in 1913?

3. Why did Caesar laugh at the pirates who kidnapped him?

4. How many semlas did King Adolf of Sweden eat before he died?

5. What was the "shame flute?"

Answers

1. 38 minutes.
2. Joseph Stalin, Leon Trotsky, Josip Broz (Tito), Sigmund Freud, and Adolf Hitler.
3. He thought he was worth more than the ransom they were asking.
4. 14.
5. It was an iron tube that a bad artist had to wear to show the public that he had disgraced his art form.

Chapter 2: True Crime

True crime isn't always about grizzly details, blood, and gore.

This chapter provides some of the strangest, and sometimes dumbest, true crime tales that you would never have thought possible.

The Self-Published Killer

A good crime book is riveting—until you find out the plot is based on a real murder, committed by the author.

Polish man Krystian Bala was a well-known, self-published author of pulp fiction. His stories always involved gruesome details of characters murdering someone, and often getting away with it.

In a 2003 novel called "Amok," Bala had the villain pulling off the kidnapping, torture, and murder of a young woman without getting caught. Three years earlier, the police had been investigating the murder of a businessman who was found by fishermen in a river. The body showed signs of torture and he was bound in a similar way to the victim in Bala's book. By 2003, however, the case had gone cold and no one at first made a connection between the murder of Dariusz Janiszewski en Bala's latest best-seller.

After getting a tipoff, police decided to look into Krystian Bala and his book with more attention. They discovered that the man who was murdered in real life was suspected of seeing Bala's ex-wife, although Bala denied knowing him.

There were also striking similarities between Bala and the character of the narrator in the book. He even gave the narrator the same name that Bala himself uses when traveling overseas.

Furthermore, Janiszewski's mobile phone was sold on an online auction four days after his murder. Police traced the sale to an account that belonged to Bala.

That clinched the case for the Polish authorities and the author was arrested in 2007 and charged with murder. He was sentenced to 25 years in jail but maintained his innocence.

He lodged an appeal, claiming he got the details in the story from press reports. In 2009, a second court dismissed his appeal and upheld his sentence.

The Killer, the Selfie, and the Blogger

Most murderers try their best to hide their crimes, but a young woman from Virginia in the U.S. did exactly the opposite. After killing who she planned to be her first victim of many, Amanda Taylor took a selfie showing the body and holding a knife, still dripping with blood, in her hand.

She was so elated about her success that she sent the selfie to a crime blogger, asking her to publish it and tell her story.

The young would-be serial killer's tale started with her fetish for murder. In her early twenties, she met a man who shared her preoccupation with all things bloody and they got married. Unfortunately, hubby Rex was also addicted to opiates.

Amanda blamed her father-in-law, Charlie Taylor, for Rex's addiction; she accused him of supplying the drugs to his son.

The pair was happy, nevertheless, and began actively fantasizing about turning into serial killers. However, before Rex could help Amanda realize her dream, his life of addiction became too much for him to handle and he committed suicide.

Amanda was furious with Charlie and decided to avenge her husband. Soon afterward, she met a man who was infatuated with her and who would do anything to please her—even help her commit murder.

Together, she and Sean Bell hatched their plan and executed it in cold blood one afternoon in April 2015. She then took the selfie before the two of them made their getaway, spending the night in a motel in Tennessee.

The blogger, who received the image and the accompanying bloodcurdling story, was appalled. Realizing that she had to try and stop the carnage, she accepted the image, but immediately contacted the police.

Charlie Taylor was to be only the first victim in a life Amanda planned for the two of them as dedicated serial killers, but the next morning, Sean had gotten cold feet. In a fit of rage, Amanda shot him in the face and left him for dead. After casually snapping a picture of his face, she took off again.

While on the run, she kept in touch with the crime blogger, who, for her part, kept the detectives informed.

Law enforcement finally caught up with Amanda in North Carolina and arrested her. Under interrogation, she happily admitted everything and asked to receive a death sentence.

After deliberating for only half an hour, a jury sentenced her to life in prison instead.

"Pay-Slipping" Into Jail

A Chicago man executed, what he thought to be, a smooth bank robbery. At 17:50 on a Friday night in 2008, he walked into a Fifth Third Bank and handed a note demanding cash to the cashier.

The cashier stayed calm and gave him all the cash available at that time—which was only about $400, but still he got some loot. He hurriedly left the bank, leaving behind his threatening note.

What the bank robber didn't realize, however, was that he had written his demand on the back of one of his own, torn pay slips. His name and address were clearly visible.

Police found the other half of the note right outside the door of the bank and had no trouble finding the culprit.

A spokesperson for the FBI later remarked that they see some fairly strange bank robberies, but few of them are so blatantly stupid.

Respectfully Yours, Goldilocks

A retired British couple returning from holiday noticed something weird when they opened the door to their house. The place was unusually tidy. The mail was collected and neatly stacked, the laundry was clean and folded, the fridge was stocked, and all the dishes were clean.

Upon further investigation, they found a 28-year-old intruder happily living in their home. Lukasz Chojnowski had settled in comfortably while they were away and was snoozing in the couple's bed when they discovered him.

The Polish-born man could not speak much English and was unable to explain his presence to the owners.

When interrogated by the police later, it turned out that he'd been evicted from his lodgings and had nowhere to go. He entered the couple's overgrown yard from the back and assumed the house was unoccupied. After breaking a window to gain entrance, the "Goldilocks intruder," as he became known, made himself at home.

In court, Chojnowski admitted to committing burglary. He received a fine and a suspended sentence. The couple later said they never felt threatened; they had, in fact, considered hiring him as a butler because he was so respectful and thorough.

A Few Floury Steps to Jail

Wearing gloves at a crime scene to avoid leaving fingerprints didn't help one careless burglar in Britain to stay out of jail.

When Somerset resident Anthony Rudkin's neighbor stepped out of his flat for a few hours, Rudkin took the opportunity to ransack the flat. He returned to his home with the neighbor's PlayStation 4 and some jewelry.

A few hours later, Rudkin got an unpleasant surprise when he opened the door and found the police waiting for him.

Rudkin had not noticed the spilled flour on the carpet in the hallway of the neighbor's flat and walked through it. Upon leaving the flat, he left a trail of white footsteps leading right up to his own front door.

A police officer from Avon and Somerset told reporters afterward that some cases of burglary require some intelligent police work, but this one... well, you decide for yourself.

The Dumpster That Should Have Been Fined

When people get traffic fines, they sometimes come up with astonishingly creative excuses.

A woman in Rhode Island, U.S. was given a ticket for parking illegally. When she appeared in court, the judge asked her to explain why she parked in a loading zone.

"Well," the woman said, "I always park legally in the spot next to the loading zone." "Oh, and why not this time?" the judge enquired.

"Because the dumpster took my parking spot, so I parked where it should have been!"

A Case of Mistaken Beverage

A low cost Canadian airline called Sunwing, prided themselves on their good in-flight service. One would assume that's why one of their packages was marketed as "champagne service."

When a traveler from Quebec by the name of Daniel Macduff booked a flight to Cuba with them, he liked the idea but took it to refer to the beverage champagne.

When he was served a cheap sparkling wine on the plane instead of real champagne, Macduff was outraged. His class action lawsuit against Sunwing for misleading advertising made international headlines.

Sunwing Airlines dismissed the case as frivolous, saying they referred to their level of service and not to a beverage. While the outcome of the court case was not widely publicized, Sunwing has since changed their advertising to state that passengers will be welcomed with a glass of sparkling wine.

IT Class for a Hacker

What do you get when you put a hacker into an IT class? More hacking, of course.

Prison authorities in the U.K. only realized their mistake after it became clear that the prison systems had been hacked.

Let's start this story from the beginning. The 21-year-old Nicholas Webber started a five-year prison sentence in 2011 for masterminding an extremely successful cybercrime site. At the tender age of 17, Webber created a site called GhostMarket. It was a forum for hackers where they could fleece unsuspecting victims from their hard-earned money.

GhostMarket, with its estimated 8,000 members worldwide, became one of the most notorious cyber fraud sites in Britain. Among other items on its menu, the site offered tips on creating computer viruses, harvesting credit card data, and it also offered details of nearly 100,000 stolen credit cards for sale.

Webber was caught when he tried to pay for hotel accommodations with stolen credit card information. Authorities calculated at the time that Webber's site could have been responsible for the loss of about £15 million ($16,805, 475).

As part of the rehabilitation program in the South London prison where Webber was sent, inmates were allowed to attend IT classes—inmates that included Webber.

After the prison system hacking was discovered during a class, the instructor told the outraged prison authorities that he had no idea who Webber was. Nevertheless, the instructor was made redundant after no other suitable employment could be found for him in the correctional services system.

A Clean Getaway That Got Hampered

On a morning in 2011, wannabe burglar Michael Trias broke into an apartment in Mesa, Arizona. His mode of entry was to jump through a bedroom window, breaking the window screen and blinds in the process.

The owner of the house was in the bathroom. When he heard the noise in the bedroom, he grabbed a broom to defend himself and went to investigate.

To his astonishment, he found a man struggling inside his clothes hamper. The hamper, made from netting and PVC, hung right below the window through which Trias jumped and the unfortunate burglar got himself helplessly tangled in the netting.

Trias faced charges of second-degree burglary, as well as criminal damage to property (including the hamper) amounting to about $100.

E-Mailed to Jail

A 19-year-old German bank robber was so proud of himself that he decided to correct the factual errors the police and press were making in reporting his crime.

He e-mailed the police to mock them that they would never catch him this way; they got his height, accent, and age wrong. They also said he escaped on foot, while he would never have dreamed of it—he had a car ready, like any self-respecting bank robber.

To his surprise, the police walked into his home just a couple of hours later and arrested him. They had traced him through the e-mail address he sent the taunting mails from.

The Parrot Murder

The New York Times reported on September 14, 1899, about the unfortunate death of a 23-year-old woman in Washington. Alice Knott was killed because of a gas leak in the room where she slept.

The murderer was apprehended at the scene. He was none other than her pet parrot.

It turns out the parrot had a particular fondness of getting high on gas. Whenever he got the chance, he pulled the gas pipes out of their fixtures and sniffed the gas until he was dizzy.

The bird was also notoriously bad-tempered and only his owner could get near him. She always rescued him from his gas fix before any harm could be done.

Being asleep the night of September 13, however, she knew nothing about his mischief. According to the news reports, the parrot realized something was wrong and made his way to the door. He pushed his beak under the door as far as he could to get some fresh air.

The parrot survived the ordeal and was caught trying to pull out another gas pipe while the coroner was still in the house.

The Robber Who Nabbed Himself

Early one morning, a 23-year-old New York man with a whole string of prior arrests to his name broke into a mini-mart in Ossining, New York. Neighbors called the police after hearing a crashing sound from the direction of the store.

The robber, Blake Leak, ran away and the police gave chase through the streets. When both cops pursuing him stumbled, he took advantage of the moment and disappeared into the grounds of a large building.

Unlucky for Leak, the large building where he sought refuge was New York's Sing Sing Maximum Security Prison. A guard spotted him and promptly apprehended him before handing him over to the police.

A Very Low High

Three house robbers thought it was their lucky day when they broke into a house in Florida, U.S. and discovered three jars containing cocaine.

Back home, they kicked back and enjoyed some of their prize. That's when they discovered they'd actually stolen three urns.

They were snorting the remains of the house owner's husband and her two dogs.

Blame the Printer

Three men in Augusta, U.S. bought a printer, but they were not happy with it. The local Target store agreed to take it back for an exchange.

When the clerk on duty checked the returned package, she found a sheet of paper in the machine with rows of counterfeit dollar bills printed on it.

The would-be easy money turned into an easy catch for police.

Caught by a Chain Reaction

Two cash strapped thieves planned to rob a cash machine to sort out their problems. Arriving at the machine, they realized they hadn't thought about how to get the money out.

They had a heavy chain in the trunk of their car and decided to try and pull the front of the machine off.

With the chain firmly attached to the front cover, they got back in the car and started pulling. The only thing that gave, however, was the bumper of their vehicle.

They left the scene without money and with the chain still attached to the cash machine. The chain also had the car bumper attached—a bumper that had the car's license plate affixed to it.

The Devil Is in the Details

Planning can make the difference between pulling off a successful crime and spending some time behind bars.

A robber in Oregon, U.S. found that out the hard way. Derrick Mosley arrived at his intended target, armed only with his trusty baseball bat.

The little detail he overlooked was that he was trying to rob a gun store. When he stormed into the shop and smashed a display cabinet with his bat, the owner of the store pulled out his own personal gun. Police arrived a few minutes later to find a motionless Mosley pinned firmly in the crosshairs.

The Dumb and Dumber Duo

Joey Miller and Matthew McNelly from Iowa, U.S. did not feel like wearing ordinary disguises to pull off their planned break-in. No ski masks or balaclavas for them; they opted for coloring their faces with black permanent marker, instead.

While it might have made it more difficult to recognize them during the break-in, permanent marker is exactly what it implies: it's very difficult to remove, especially from skin.

It made the police's job much easier; they just had to look for two clowns with black lines on their faces.

Say What?

In 1995, a Berlin man named Klaus Schmidt entered a bank, brandishing a gun and demanding money.

The tellers immediately responded, and everything seemed to be going according to plan, until one teller asked Schmidt, "Do you want a bag?"

Schmidt responded with, "You're damn right, this is a real gun!"

The tellers then realized that Schmidt was deaf. They activated the bank's alarm without him being any wiser.

Great was his surprise when the police walked in to arrest him.

In an interesting twist, Schmidt later sued the bank for exploiting his disability.

Daylight Robbery?!

James Blankenship from Ohio, U.S. decided to break into his own mother's home. He was banned from her house after a quarrel earlier that year.

It was broad daylight and Blankenship's mother caught him trying to get in. He ran away while she phoned the police.

While searching for him, a neighbor told the officers he had seen a man running behind one of the nearby houses. Upon closer investigation, they found Blankenship hiding in the crawl space of the house and arrested him.

He was, however, highly indignant about this treatment. He was under the impression he couldn't get arrested for breaking and entering, because it was daytime; in his book, it was only a criminal offense when committed during the night.

Clowning Around

When you choose a disguise for a robbery, it should be something that should blend in with the crowds as you make your getaway.

A blonde wig, fake breasts, and a pair of bright clown's pants definitely don't fit this bill.

To Pennsylvania man Dennis Hawkins it seemed like the perfect outfit for a bank robbery in his hometown.

He first stopped at a toy shop and stole a toy gun before heading to the bank—completely forgetting that he did not shave his beard off. The anomaly of the beard and the fake breasts already blew his cover before he even got started.

After getting the money, Hawkins went outside and opened one of the money packets. The red dye inside exploded, staining him. Looking more bizarre by the moment, he tried to get a lift from motorists at a nearby gas station.

When everyone refused, he got into a woman's car and demanded that she take him where he wanted to go. She calmly got out of the car, removed her keys and went to the nearest police station.

Officers found him a couple of minutes later still sitting in the car.

The Polite Thief

Politeness does not always pay off, as in the case of a 36-year-old man who wanted to rob a bank in Salt Lake City in the U.S.

He arrived at the bank before it opened one morning and waited patiently in the queue for his turn to go in. The only problem is, he was already wearing a ski mask and a hoodie, with the hood pulled up over his head.

When he reached a teller, he made his demand for money. Several customers who had been queueing with him, tackled him. All the police had to do was take him away.

Bonus Interrogation

Quiz Corner

1. What did the "Selfie Killer" post on her social media?
2. How did a dumpster cause a motorist to get a parking fine?
3. How did a jailed U.K. hacker manage to hack the prison system?
4. What was a parrot's method of murder on September 14, 1899?
5. How did the cash machine robbers get caught by a chain?

Answers

1. A bloodied knife and a dead body.

2. The motorist always parked in the spot where the dumpster had been put, so the motorist left his car in the loading bay where the dumpster should have been, as a form of protest.

3. He was allowed to attend an IT class for inmates.

4. The bird pulled a gas pipe free while his owner was sleeping in a bedroom with the door closed.

5. They attached the chain to the front of the machine, but their car bumper, with the license plate, came off and stayed behind.

Are you enjoying my BOOK?

At the risk of interrupting your reading experience and potentially coming across as a bit of a bother (which I truly do hope I am not), I would love to know if you are enjoying the read so far? If so, this is fabulous news! A great deal of work goes into anything I produce, and as a full-time author, reviews are the foundation of my livelihood. I rely on them as a "green light" for other readers who may consider giving mine a whirl. So, to aid in my quest for more "book whirling," I hope you might review this one.

If so, I will take it as a virtual "high five!" And to make the process easier, I have listed the direct review links below.

U.S: https://bit.ly/EPICTRUETALES_US

Cananda: https://bit.ly/EPICTRUETALES_CA

U.K: https://bit.ly/EPICTRUETALES_UK

Australia: https://bit.ly/EPICTRUETALES_AU

If you have decided that my book is worthwhile, thank you.

Chapter 3: The Famous and Their Little Secrets

Just when you think there's nothing new to learn about your favorite actor or singer, a book like this comes along.

Hold on to your hats, some of the stories in this chapter are pretty crazy.

Strange Steve

Apple co-founder and former CEO, Steve Jobs, had a strange relationship with food. His biography paints a picture of a man who was not afraid to try new diets.

He would sometimes eat only one or two things for weeks at a time. His co-workers recalled him "looking like a sunset" after eating only carrots, and nothing else, for several weeks.

Before turning to full veganism, Jobs tried a type of veganism called fruitarianism. On this diet, every part of a plant that can be eaten without harming the growth of the plant is consumed.

Jobs then settled on veganism in general but misunderstood the effect of the diet in some respects. He was of the opinion that a vegan diet would reduce the production of mucus in the body, therefore all body odors would be eliminated. He stopped wearing deodorants and showered only occasionally. According to ex-colleagues that were interviewed for the biography, Jobs was sadly mistaken about the body odor. The limited nutrients provided by a vegan diet actually slow down the body's detoxification process, exacerbating body odor.

Elvis' Bodyguard Brother

The one and only king of rock 'n' roll had an identical twin brother. Unfortunately, the little boy was stillborn, 35 minutes before Elvis Aaron Presley was born.

Although the singer grew up as an only child, he always spoke about his twin brother, who was called Jesse Garon. He regarded Jesse as his spiritual guide and his "original bodyguard."

Bright as Well as Pretty

An actor with academic achievements equally as impressive as her acting talents is Natalie Portman.

After finishing school, she obtained a bachelor's degree in psychology from Harvard University. A paper she wrote during that time on debunking a new method of lie detection is still used in the psychology department.

After becoming a research assistant to psychology professor Alan Dershowitz, Portman also co-authored a published paper called "Frontal Lobe Activation during Object Permanence: Data from Near-Infrared Spectroscopy."

The Big Spender

Hollywood actor Nicholas Cage was once the highest earning actor of all time, according to Forbes. Between 1996 and 2011, he earned more than $150 million. The year 2009 alone netted him a cool $40 million.

Unfortunately, he was prone to making hugely expensive and sometimes slightly crazy purchases. His buys include a 67-million-year-old Tarbosaurus skull bought at $300,000, two islands in the Bahamas, four luxury yachts, of which the most expensive had 12 master bedrooms and set him back $20 million, a famous haunted house in New Orleans, a collection of shrunken pygmy heads, a nine foot tall tombstone in the shape of a pyramid, a crocodile, a shark, an octopus, a Gulfstream jet, 15 luxury homes, and two medieval castles.

After ending up broke and with a $13 million fine from the IRS, Cage sold most of these purchases to get out of debt.

No Dirty Spoons, Please!

Singer Liam Payne makes no bones about his spoon phobia; specifically, of other people's dirty spoons.

He revealed that his koutaliaphobia, as an irrational fear of spoons is known, came from his school days.

The naughty kids at the school he attended were punished with a stint at washing dishes. Payne said the images of the dirty spoons he had to clean, without knowing what the kids did with them, stuck in his mind and turned into a phobia.

Feet First

Tennis players are notorious for their superstitions and the great Serena Williams is no exception. It is, however, interesting to note that all her superstitions involve her feet.

She is adamant that her tennis shoes have to be tied in a certain way. After some of the losses during her career, she publicly blamed the fact that her shoes were laced the wrong way.

She also believes in bringing her shower sandals with her to the tennis court before every match.

Another one of her eccentric beliefs is about her socks. If she is on a winning streak, she keeps on wearing the same pair of unwashed socks for every match.

From Bug-Knocker to Superstar

Today, Taylor Swift is one of the most successful female pop artists in the world. As a kid, however, her job in the family's part-time business was to knock bugs from Christmas trees.

Her family lived on a Christmas tree farm in Pennsylvania, U.S. The praying mantises loved building their pods in the pine trees. Little Taylor, who was too young to help lift trees onto customers' vehicles, had to knock all the pods out before the tree was collected to prevent the insects from hatching in the people's houses.

Never Too Young for Big Business

Warren Buffett's success story in the financial world and investing started when he was 10.

As a kid in elementary school, he regularly lunched with a member of the New York Stock Exchange. While other children his age were thinking about baseball and reading comics, he discussed stocks with his lunch partner.

Buffett bought his first stocks at age 11 for $38 apiece. By the time he turned 16, he had already accumulated more than $53,000 from his investments and other side businesses he had started.

As of 2022, his net worth is $98.8 billion. Most of that wealth was only acquired after he turned 60.

Typing Tom

American actor Tom Hanks, famous for roles like Forrest Gump, has a passion for typewriters. Specifically, really old typewriters.

He has a collection of more than 100 of the old machines. When asked about the reason behind his fascination with typewriters, he said that, for him, nothing beats the feeling of really hitting the keys—a completely different experience to politely tapping on a computer keyboard.

Bean Power

Rowan Atkinson, the British actor best known for his comic role as Mr. Bean, does not only break things. He can also fix them, because he is a qualified electrical engineer.

Atkinson obtained his bachelor's degree in electrical engineering from Newcastle University in 1974. He started his master's degree the next year but did not complete it because he made his comedy debut at the BBC in the popular show "Not the nine-o-clock-news."

The Queen's College, Oxford, made Atkinson an Honorary Fellow in 2006.

A Firm Footing

Socialite, model, and businesswoman Paris Hilton is used to being scrutinized by the public, from head to toe. There is, however, one part of her body that she would have preferred to be skipped: her size 11 feet.

In her memoirs published in 2021, she jokes about her shoe problems with such big feet. Referring to the stylish flat shoes popular now, she said she couldn't wear them without looking like she had canoes on her feet.

Tesla's Strange Habits

Serbian-born Nikola Tesla is renowned for astute scientific thinking that was far ahead of his time.

Few people, however, know that he also had a couple of phobias and strange habits—possibly because he was such an intensely emotional genius.

One of his phobias was about pearls. He refused to speak to women wearing pearl jewelry. If his secretary turned up for work wearing anything with pearls, he sent her home for the day.

He intensely disliked earrings and made no secret of his aversion whenever he encountered a woman wearing a pair.

Tesla suffered from obsessive-compulsive disorder and felt himself compelled to do everything in threes. He would, for example, only accept hotel rooms that could be divided by three. His daily swim had to be done in 33 laps. If he lost count, he started over until he knew he had completed 33 rounds. He often circled a block three times before entering a building. When leaving a building, he had to turn right and circle the building before he felt free to leave.

He was obsessed with pigeons and even claimed to have fallen in love with one.

Dinner had to be at 20:10 sharp every night. His obsession with germs had him polishing every piece of cutlery to a shine. He also demanded three folded napkins per course of food, using 18 napkins every night.

Before starting his meal, he estimated the weight of the food. He said he couldn't enjoy dinner if he did not do that. He also counted his chewing movements.

Before going to bed, he curled the toes of each foot 100 times, claiming that it stimulated his brain.

He intensely hated touching hair and refused to shake hands with anyone.

He lived out his last days until his death at age 86 in poverty, in room 3327 on the 33rd floor of the New Yorker Hotel.

Bonus Interrogation

1. Which item of clothing did Steve Jobs not change regularly?
2. How much money did Nicholas Cage burn through in a short time?
3. What does Liam Payne have a phobia about?
4. At what age did Warren Buffett buy his first stocks?
5. About which body part is Paris Hilton self-conscious?

Answers

1. His socks.
2. $150 million.
3. Dirty spoons.
4. 11.
5. Her feet.

Chapter 4: Inventions

Without the great minds of inventors, the world would be a vastly different place to live. All the discoveries and inventions are important elements of the fabric of our society—but what about the inventions that never really took off?

In this chapter, we'll explore some of the kookiest inventions in history. You might find yourself asking, "What were they thinking?!"

The Radio Hat

Long before the invention of headphones, AirPods, and Bluetooth speakers, there was the portable radio hat. The invention even had several incarnations.

The first mention of such a hat came from the early 1920s, but it didn't seem to attract many customers. The large straw hat with two antennas poking out was remarkably similar to the invention that hit the news in 1930. At that time, radios were bulky pieces of furniture, and the inventors used the portability of their headgear as their marketing hook.

Neither version made much of an impression, however. It was only in 1949 that a novelty store in Brooklyn had some success selling their "Man From Mars Radio Hat."

Radio hats disappeared completely from the market in 1955 with the invention of transistor radios.

Wooden Swimwear

You could be forgiven if the idea of a wooden bathing suit gave you a sinking feeling—pardon the pun.

Swimwear made from spruce veneer was the brainchild of the lumber producing Grays Harbor County in Washington State. The area was, and still is, famous for its timber industry.

The wood producers launched an advertising campaign in 1929 featuring ladies known as the "Spruce Girls." They held a "wood week" in the summer of that year with the Spruce Girls frolicking in the sea and posing on the beach, wearing their bathing suits made from thin spruce veneer.

The advertisers described the swimwear as cheap, quick to make, and fashionable. They also believed the veneer had a high enough buoyancy that timid swimmers could be persuaded to take a dip when wearing such a suit.

Nobody knows whether the suits were really as comfortable to wear as the designers claimed and they disappeared quickly from the fashion scene.

The Smile Computer

In 2009, a private Japanese railroad company was so adamant that their employees had to welcome customers with a friendly face that they turned to a computer to analyze their morning smiles.

The Japanese technology company OMRON designed special software they described as "smile degree estimation." Every one of the more than 500 employees of the Keihin Electric Express Railway Company (now known as the Keikyu Corporation) had to grin at a camera connected to the computer, first thing after arriving at work.

The software measured the smile, taking things like the curve of the lips and the amount of crinkling around the eyes into account. A score out of 100 was awarded, after which the computer weighed in with feedback.

It dispatched sage advice such as, “lift up the corners of your mouth,” “smile wider, you look serious,” or, “smile like you’re really feeling happy.”

Although it’s anyone’s guess whether the rail company is still using the application, OMRON is still marketing its software as Image Sensing technology. They updated it in 2013 to measure seven different facial expressions that employers might find useful to identify in their workforce: neutrality, fear, sadness, happiness, surprise, anger, and disgust.

The Laid Back Piano

A couple of British inventors decided in 1935 that being bedridden for whatever reason is no excuse for missing piano practice. They designed a portable keyboard they called an "invalid piano."

It consisted of a box-like contraption that stood at the end of the bed, housing a keyboard that could extend on foldable arms toward the player's hands. The keyboard itself looked much like a modern electronic keyboard, although it was just bulkier.

Unfortunately, the remarkable instrument survived only in images kept in a collection in the Netherlands.

Transport Fit for a Criminal

In the early 1920s, police did not have squad cars to chase criminals and transport them to jail. They mostly made use of motorcycles.

To solve the problem of secure transport for an arrested person, police bikes were fitted with sidecars that were enclosed with bars.

Unfortunately, the mobile holding cells were more top-heavy than anticipated, making the motorcycle difficult to drive. It was also dangerous for the driver to try and control the bike if a prisoner did not sit still, so the trend did not last very long.

Big on Fresh Air, Not So Big on Safety

Making sure your baby gets enough fresh air is a good thing, but not if that means the baby has to dangle several floors above the ground.

That apparently did not bother the American health worker Mrs. Robert C. Lafferty. She patented a window baby cage in 1913, to help parents living in apartments without gardens, to get their offspring some fresh air. The cage was clamped to a window frame, and it rested on the windowsill.

She called her wire contraption a health crib, designed it as a 2 x 2 x 2.5-feet box with padding at the bottom. It had a solid roof to keep incontinent pigeons away from the baby.

It might not come as a surprise to you that Ms. Lafferty had no children of her own.

Slug Power

Are you tired of slugs destroying your garden? The inventors of the slugbot believe they have solved the problem.

In 2001, AI scientists from the California Institute of Technology unveiled a little robot that seeks out and destroys slugs.

The gadget is equipped with a light to locate slugs when crawling through the garden. When an invader is spotted, it is picked up and placed inside the bot. Special bacteria digest the slug and the organic residue is used to power the slugbot.

Butterface

A company in Vermont, U.S., in 2014 invented customized toasters for bread with a view.

The appliance uses a photo to guide heat along a metal plate, resulting in a likeness of whatever is on the photo to get burned onto the toast.

That means you could use a photo of yourself to get a really personalized slice of bread. It puts a whole new spin on buttering yourself up!

A Human Roomba

You don't normally associate a baby with cleaning; rather the opposite, mostly. Junior can, however, start doing a share of the housework when wearing the mop onesie.

A company in New York started marketing rompers with mop heads sewn to the arms and legs. As the baby crawls, the mops pick up dirt and lint while polishing the floor.

The inspiration for the invention came from a Japanese spoof ad from the late 1990s.

Cloud Sourcing

You can apply this headline literally to the smart umbrella.

The first version of the gadget called a HAZ was designed in 2017 by a South Korean startup. The motorized umbrella boasts several features, all based on its built-in Bluetooth connectivity.

The smart umbrella will alert you through location tracking if you accidentally leave it behind, showing you on your smartphone exactly where it is waiting for you.

While walking outside with it, the umbrella will connect to weather networks and other smart umbrellas to get the latest information about the clouds and expected precipitation. It will also measure UV levels and alert you if they go dangerously high.

Calling Apple Fans

No need to suffer the heat anymore while using your iPhone. In 2018, Apple patented a minute fan that plugs into the charging socket.

The head pivots so browsing remains comfortable at all times. The small micro motor is powerful enough to cause enough wind to cool the phone user.

Although the little fans are still being sold online and in Apple stores, many users have complained in online forums about the gadget damaging the phone's battery.

A Tip Requester

Are you a chronically shy waiter or porter? No problem, if you have Russel E. Oakes' 1955 invention around your waist.

Oakes designed an artificial hand requesting a tip, with a cashbox attached, that could be strapped around the waist. The hand was worn behind the person's back.

When a tip was placed in the hand, the cashbox registered a receipt. If the tip was deemed too low, the display said "No sale."

The Pedestrian Catcher

In the 1930s, cars were still novelties on the roads and pedestrians were frequently knocked down. Car companies tried to outdo each other to find a solution to the problem.

Two young designers from Sheffield, U.K. came up with the pedestrian catcher, aka the safety scoop. It consisted of something looking like a roll-up hammock on wheels, mounted to the front of the car. The hammock could be stored inside the front bumper or replace the bumper altogether.

The driver only had to flick a lever to unroll the hammock and scoop up the person who strayed into the road. The catcher would then gently roll the person along while the driver slows down, so the pedestrian could get up and live to walk another day.

It didn't catch on, though, because not all drivers were alert enough to deploy the catcher in time.

Bonus Interrogation

1. In which country were smile checks implemented?
2. How did police transport criminals in the 1920s?
3. Which 1913 invention claimed to give babies in the cities a chance of getting fresh air?
4. What is the slugbot?
5. How did car manufacturers in the 1930s try to minimize pedestrian accidents?

Answers

1.

2. Japan.

3. Their motorcycles had sidecars with bars, forming mobile cells.

4. The baby cage that was hung out over the window sills of apartment buildings.

5. A little robot that seeks out and kills slugs in the garden.

6. They invented the pedestrian catcher, to be fitted on the front of vehicles.

Chapter 5: Stretching the Truth: Hoaxes and Scams

Hoaxes, fake news, and scams are nothing new. They predate the internet by far, although they're much easier to spread these days.

Some of these stories have become so ingrained in our collective consciousness that it might come as a shock to discover they were never true.

A Cartoon With Staying Power

In 1803, a British cartoonist named James Gillray published a cartoon of the French general Napoleon Bonaparte. That in itself was nothing unusual—Gillray made fun of Napoleon regularly.

This was, however, the first time the Frenchman was portrayed as being small in stature. The cartoon entitled "Maniac-ravings or Little Boney in a strong fit," satirized an angry outburst from

Napoleon which took place on March 14, 1803, at the Tuileries palace in Paris and shocked the diplomatic world. Napoleon launched a ferocious verbal attack on Lord Whitworth, the British ambassador, about the conduct of the English government, before stomping off to his apartments.

The image of Napoleon being a short, angry, and boastful man stuck and is being perpetuated to this day.

The truth was that the French emperor was probably of average height. Although he is said to have measured only 5 feet 2 inches, the French inch in use at the time was longer than the English inch. That puts him at a height of 5 feet 5 inches. That was only about an inch shorter than the average male height during the period.

Napoleon himself said, at the end of his life, that James Gillray had been more effective in bringing him down than all the European armies.

A Garden Shed With a Reputation

In 2017, a brand new London restaurant became the top-rated dining establishment on the travel website TripAdvisor in just five months. "The Shed at Dulwich" was a boutique eatery, operating by appointment only. According to the website, the chef cooked to match his patrons' moods.

The waiting list to get in was six months long and growing. Enthusiastic reviews about the "mind-blowingly good" food and unbeatable ambience flooded the internet and everybody who was somebody tried to get a reservation.

The only problem was that the restaurant did not exist.

Freelance journalist Oobah Butler wanted to see if he could sway public opinion on social media with nothing more than advertising, so he began marketing the garden shed where he lived as a posh restaurant. He bought a cheap phone for the number he supplied in the ad, created a website, and launched his hoax. He published stylized images of plates of food that looked mouthwatering and enlisted the help of friends and family to post raving reviews.

When he admitted his prank to the world a few weeks later, he revealed that the supposed food in the images were concoctions thrown together using household supplies such as sponges, shaving foam, runny honey, and bleach tablets.

To see how far he could take his social experiment before telling all, he opened the Shed for one night to real diners. The people, who thought they had scored the hottest reservation on the planet, were met at a vague address in the street and taken blindfolded to the venue.

Inside, they were served warmed-up microwave dinners while sipping cheap wine from very ordinary mugs and having only paper napkins to use. A mediocre DJ played music at strategic times to mask the sound of the microwave warming up the food in the house.

Afterward, every patron was asked individually what they thought of the evening. All of them said they loved the unique experience and the novel concept and would definitely be back.

So much for independent opinion forming!

Monkeying Around with Art

At a prestigious art exhibition in Göteborg, Sweden in February 1964, critics were almost unanimous in their praise for the works of a new French artist. Pierre Brassau painted in avant-garde style with vibrant splotches of color.

Praise for Brassau's work ranged from "determined," and "extremely detailed," to "delicate like a ballet dancer."

Only one critic was not impressed. In his judgment, the paintings looked like an ape had done them.

He was, in fact, the only one who came close to the truth. Pierre Brassau was a four-year-old West African chimpanzee from a Swedish zoo, named Peter.

Journalist Åke "Dacke" Axelsson wanted to see if art critics could be fooled by paintings done by someone or something other than a human. He persuaded the chimpanzee's keeper to give him canvases, paint brushes, and oil paints.

At first, Peter preferred to eat the paints. Eventually he started coloring the canvases and Pierre Brassau was born.

When Axelsson revealed his hoax after the exhibition, one of the critics still insisted that it was the best painting of all.

Internet Browsers and Intelligence

In July 2011, internet users were in a commotion about a report claiming that people using the Internet Explorer browser had lower intelligence than those using other browsers.

A company called AptiQuant Psychometric Consulting Company released the findings to the press, and news outlets from the U.S. and U.K. immediately ran with the story.

The researchers reportedly compared the IQs of 100,000 browser users and correlated that data with the specific browser each participant in the study preferred. Internet Explorer fans allegedly scored significantly lower in the intelligence department than the others.

A month later, the creator of the bogus report confessed to it being a hoax. Tarandeep Gill, a Canadian web developer, explained that he wanted to create awareness of the number of outdated versions of Internet Explorer that were around.

If nothing else, in retrospect, the speed with which the international press accepted the story seemed to suggest a slight anti-Microsoft sentiment to some analysts.

The Mythical King of the Middle Ages

During the Middle Ages, the Muslim world and the European Christians were often at war with each other. When spirits started flagging, the commanders tried anything to boost their troops' morale—including inventing inspirational characters such as Prester John.

His name was first recorded in 1145, when a scribe wrote it down during a meeting between Hugh, Bishop of Jabala in Syria and Pope Eugenius III. The bishop did not bring good news; he told the Pope about the Muslim victory in Edessa the previous year.

The city of Edessa was located in the southeastern region of what is known as Turkey today. It represented an important conquest for the Christian Crusaders from which they started evangelizing Mesopotamia and Persia.

The Crusader soldiers badly needed some encouragement, so the legend of John the Priest (Prester John) was born. He was pictured as a great Christian power in the east who was on his way to help the Crusaders.

The last mention of his name was in the 17th century. Several explorers and adventurers had been looking for him and his fabled wealthy kingdom, purportedly locating him somewhere in Africa.

Even after it became clear in the 1500s that Prester John did not really exist, the myth lived on. The story inspired many writers, including Shakespeare, Umberto Eco, and John Buchan.

The Ultimate April Fool's Joke

The butt of this hoax was the prestigious Louvre museum in Paris, France. The management of the museum announced triumphantly on April 1, 1896, that they had acquired a priceless golden tiara that had belonged to King Saitaphernes of Scythia, a kingdom in eastern Europe.

The tiara looked like a cone-shaped hat, decorated with scenes from Homer's "Iliad," as well as depicting the daily lives of Scythians. It also featured a Greek inscription saying that the people of Olbia wished to honor the great king with the magnificent golden headdress.

The seller of the artifact, Schapschelle Hochmann, claimed that the tiara was made in the 3rd century B.C.E. The date made sense to the experts at the Louvre. According to history, King Saitaphernes besieged the Greek colony of Olbia at the time. He was eventually persuaded to lift the siege and spare the city in exchange for lavish gifts.

The crown was proudly exhibited in the museum from 1896 to 1903. International archaeologists, however, soon started questioning the authenticity of the item. They were specifically bothered by the amazingly preserved state of the tiara. There was only slight damage and solely in non-essential areas.

After a very public six-year-long debate, the curators of the Louvre agreed to do a thorough investigation. To their huge embarrassment, the crown proved to be fake.

In the late 1800s, Schapschelle Hochmann and his brother Leiba approached a talented goldsmith in the Ukrainian city of Odessa to make the tiara for an archaeological friend of theirs. They gave the smith, Israel Rouchomovsky, detailed instructions and provided books with illustrations of the scenes they wanted as decorations on the piece.

Without informing Rouchomovsky of their intentions, the brothers then set about trying to sell the fake tiara to museums. A friend of Rouchomovsky who was around while he was making it, saw the piece in the Louvre by chance and told Rouchomovsky about it.

Although Rouchomovsky was outraged at first at being duped, the scandal resulted in bringing him much fame and fortune. He moved his wife and children to Paris and enjoyed a hugely successful career until his death in 1934.

A Furry Fishy Story

The 2015 image of a fur-covered trout, allegedly caught by a fisherman in Wisconsin in the U.S. had some people fooled for several years.

That was, however, not the first time the alleged fur-covered animal came to the world's attention.

A museum in Colorado was previously caught out in the 1930s for someone having supplied them with three furry fish, as well as a bogus scientist who claimed to study the phenomenon.

The Royal Museum of Scotland also had a furry specimen proudly displayed on their wall in the 1950s, until a Canadian taxidermist admitted to wrapping the fish in rabbit fur before presenting it to the museum.

An Onion Charger

In 2008, a YouTube video showing an iPod purportedly being charged with an onion was viewed more than seven million times.

The video was made by a person with the alias of "Household Hacker." According to the instructions, a small white onion had to be soaked in Gatorade until it had absorbed all the electrolytes in the energy drink.

The USB charger was then plugged into the onion and, according to the video, the iPod would spring to life.

The procedure was debunked later that same year on the TV show "MythBusters," on Discovery Channel. The co-host of the program, Adam Savage, explained that even if the onion could absorb enough electrolytes to conduct electricity, there were no pathways for the electricity to follow to the iPod's battery.

Spaghetti Trees

Forget about money growing on trees; spaghetti does, however. Or so a BBC news show convinced its viewers in 1957.

As an April Fool's joke, the "Panorama" show aired a three minute-clip showing a Swiss family allegedly harvesting abundant strands of spaghetti from their spaghetti trees.

Many of the estimated eight million people who saw the video were fooled. The next day, the BBC was inundated with calls from viewers wanting to know how they could grow their own spaghetti trees. The BBC's whimsical advice to the callers was to place a sprig of spaghetti in a tin of tomato sauce and hope for the best.

Dark Times Ahead?

A hoax that keeps on cropping up every few years is one seemingly featuring a NASA director warning that the earth is about to go dark for six days. It first made the rounds on the Internet in 2012.

In the December 2020 version, NASA director Charles Bolden (who had already resigned in 2017) warned people to prepare for all emergencies because the earth was about to experience total darkness between December 16 and December 22, 2020.

The hoax was debunked the first time, but its 2020 remake included Bolden. NASA later said Bolden had talked about being prepared for possible emergencies, but it was meant in general terms and never mentioned a blackout.

No Bathtub for the President

American president Millard Fillmore didn't use a bathtub. Not because he neglected his personal hygiene, but because he didn't have a bathtub—despite the fake news claiming he installed the first bathtub in America.

In 1917, the world was a depressing place. WWI was making people gloomy, and the writer H. L. Mencken decided to cheer up his fellow Americans with a feel-good story.

He proclaimed December 20 as the anniversary of the arrival of the bathtub in America, in a long essay published in the New York Evening Mail. According to his story, bathrooms didn't really catch on with the American public until Fillmore installed one, complete with a bathtub, in the White House.

Mencken thought everyone would see through the joke, but to his huge surprise, the fake information was believed widely. A few years later, it was even cited in learned journals and reference was made to it in Congress.

Mencken's efforts to convince the world he merely intended some harmless fun fell on deaf ears. The bogus fact was mentioned as late as 2008 in a Kia ad.

The Wild West for Tourists

The small Nevada town of Palisade was a really peaceful place in 1868. They didn't even need a sheriff, and everyone got on just fine.

When the Transcontinental Railroad opened in 1869, passing through Palisade, tourists started talking about the town—but not in a positive way. According to town records, passing passengers expressed disappointment to the train conductor because there were no spectacular Wild West-style fights to be seen.

To boost visits to their town, the residents started staging gun fights in the streets and bank robberies. Everybody was in on the hoax, even the US Cavalry as well as a nearby Native American tribe.

The show was abandoned after a couple of years, but Palisade made a place in history for themselves.

Bonus Interrogation

1. Was Napoleon really short?

2. True or false: "The Shed at Dulwich" was an exclusive restaurant.

3. Was the famously wealthy Prester John a real king in history?

4. With which item were the curators of the Louvre duped in 1896?

5. Which vegetable can be used to charge an iPod, according to a 2008 YouTube video?

Answers

1. No, his real height was 5 feet 6 inches.

2. False. It was a hoax, with the perpetrator naming the fake restaurant after the backyard garden shed he was living in.

3. No, the legend of Prester John was created to boost the flagging spirits of the Crusader soldiers.

4. A fake golden tiara.

5. An onion.

Chapter 6: Sport and Sports

Humans are beings who play whenever they get a chance and sport is an illustration of our love for games.

A select few individuals really excel at their chosen sport, reaching astonishing heights.

Then there are those guys who are just out to have a good time while playing...

The Magic of Jesse Owens

There is a specific 45-minute period in 1935 that has become known as the "magical 45 minutes of sport."

It happened on May 25, 1935, which was the day of the Big Ten Championships. Being a leading intercollegiate athletics meet in the U.S. the athletes getting ready to compete were world class.

The 21-year-old Jesse Owens was widely expected to do well. Unbeknownst to his fans though, his coach nearly pulled him out of the event. Five days earlier, Owens fell down the stairs in his dormitory. His lower back sustained serious bruising. According to reports, he had to be helped into and out of the car taking him to the venue. He was unable to touch his toes when he bent down, so he took a hot bath before going out onto the track to try and loosen up his stiff muscles.

His coach finally agreed to let him take part, but he had to be assessed after each event.

Owens proceeded to break three world records and equaled one other during the next 45 minutes. He cleared hurdles, sprinted, and jumped himself into history with records that stood unchallenged for many years.

Winter and Summer Are Not Equal

The Olympic athletes of the principality of Liechtenstein found this out the hard way.

Liechtenstein is a small, German-speaking stretch of land between Austria and Switzerland. At about 62 square miles, it is one of the smallest countries in Europe. About two-thirds of the country forms part of the Alpine mountains.

Although the climate is mild, with winter temperatures seldom falling below 5 degrees Fahrenheit, the mountainous terrain ensures that Liechtenstein can boast a number of good skiers.

This helped the country to win 10 medals at the Winter Olympics since they first joined the International Olympic Committee in 1935. Both in population and area, Liechtenstein is the smallest country to have done so well in the Winter Olympics.

They could, however, not equal the feat in the Summer Olympics. They hold the somewhat dubious record of being the only country that has never won any medals in any Summer Olympics.

Proving a Point on the Tennis Court

The longest point ever played in a tennis match lasted 29 minutes.

On September 24, 1984, the first rounds of the Virginia Slims-sponsored Ginny tournament in Richmond, Virginia were being played. Vicki Nelson Dunbar and Jean Hepner were battling it out on the court.

Neither player wanted to concede any points and they kept lobbing the ball back and forth, no matter how hard their opponent tried to catch them out.

When Nelson Dunbar finally bested Hepner for the coveted point, 29 minutes had passed. The rally saw 643 shots being played.

By the time Nelson Dunbar wrapped up the match with 6-4, 7-6, it was six-and-a-half hours later. For 20 years, this remained the longest match played in tennis history. It still is the longest match to be completed in one single day.

A Competition That Could Make You Sleepy

You could be forgiven if you thought the annual Australian sheep counting competition was about a good night's rest.

Contestants, however, literally count sheep. The first championship was held in 2002, in New South Wales.

The rules are simple; about 400 sheep madly dash past the competitors and they have to try and count them accurately.

The first winner was Peter Desailly, who correctly counted 277 sheep.

When asked why the Aussies want to hold sheep counting championships, some of the entrants explained that they saw it as a good way to bring an edge and some interest to their daily grind of farm work.

Worm Wisdom

Strange sports events are not the exclusive domain of Australians; the residents of Cheshire, in the U.K., give them a good go with their World Worm Charming Championship. The competition started in 1980 and has since become a much-loved annual event.

Competitors have to coax as many earthworms as they can from their allotted patch of ground during a half-hour period. Absolutely no digging is allowed—the worms have to be "called" by raising vibrations in the ground. Sticking a garden fork into the soil and banging on the tines is one of the most popular methods used by successful charmers.

After careful extraction, the worms are placed in buckets filled with moist compost to be counted after the competition. The winner receives the Golden Worm trophy.

The current record is held by a ten-year-old girl. In 2009, she charmed 567 worms from her 3 x 3 yds patch.

Chicken Nuggets for World Records

Jamaican athlete Usain Bolt made the world sit up and take notice of him during the 2008 Beijing Summer Olympics. He broke three world records and cemented his place as one of the greatest sprinters of all time.

Upon arriving in the Olympic village however, Bolt realized after his first meal that he might have a problem. He later told reporters that the food did not taste like the Chinese food sold in the West at all, and his body did not react to it well.

The only food he could recognize, and depend on for its taste and ingredients, were chicken nuggets. Because he wanted to do well in the Games, he decided to make the little balls of crumbed chicken the sole ingredient of his diet for the duration of his stay in Beijing.

According to Bolt, he consumed about 1,000 of McDonald's Chicken McNuggets in 10 days and drank only bottled water.

The chicken formula worked great for the Jamaican's performance. Apparently he still loves chicken to this day!

Who Said Archers Need Arms?

American archer Matt Stutzman holds a world record for hitting his mark at the longest distance under Olympic conditions. During the World Archery Para Championships in 2015, Stutzman succeeded with a shot of 930 feet.

The most extraordinary aspect of this remarkable feat is that he was born without arms. At four months old, he was adopted into a family of avid hunters in Iowa. He wanted to be like his father and brothers and his father bought his first bow for him when he turned 16.

The bow sits on his right shoulder, and he draws it with his right leg. A mechanical release mechanism is located under his jaw bone. He fires the arrow by moving his jaw slightly backward with about as much pressure as it takes to use a computer mouse.

Legal Shin-Kicking

The small English town of Chipping Campden, in Gloucestershire, has a proud tradition that started in 1612. The Cotswold Olimpick Games have been held there as regularly as possible during the more than 400 years of the Games' existence.

A 17th century lawyer by the name of Robert Dover, who was known as a jovial and generous man, popular in all walks of life, created the sport as an alternative form of wrestling. Dover also masterminded the Olimpick Games and is depicted on horseback as the master of ceremonies in a 1636 pamphlet about the Cotswold Games.

Besides regular events such as tug-of-war, wrestling, and horse racing, the Games are also the home of competitive shin-kicking. Competitors grab each other by the shirt lapels and try to get enough kicks into their opponent's shins to send them to the ground.

Although the general goal of the competition seems to be fun and mayhem, there are a couple of (widely-defined) rules to follow. This has led to the British newspaper "The Daily Mail" labeling it "Britain's stupidest sport."

What's in a Name?

The game of soccer is one of the most popular in the world. According to estimates by international sports bodies, there are more than 240 million registered players worldwide. Their supporters number in the billions.

Have you ever wondered why the game is called soccer?

It turns out the word evolved from student slang in the 1800s. The players of this new ball game were in football associations at universities. At the time, there were few differences between football (rugby) and soccer.

When the rules of soccer were formalized in 1863, soccer players were incorporated into an association of their own. Rugby and soccer became known, respectively, as rugby football and association football.

The abbreviation for the word "association" is "assoc." Students shortened the abbreviation even more to "socca." The addition of the "-er" suffix was following the trend at Cambridge and Oxford to add the suffix to many words, such as rugger for rugby.

As time went by and the English lost their preoccupation with American culture that started after WWII, the preferred word in Britain once again became "football."

On Your Marks, Ready, Slow!

That is indeed the case at the annual snail racing championship in Norfolk, England. The current World Snail Racing Championships winner, Sammy, covered the 13-inch track in 2 minutes and 38 seconds.

The fastest champion on record was Archie, who won the event in 1995 in two minutes flat. Archie even secured a place in the Guinness Book of World Records for himself.

The championship was started in the 1960s by an eccentric farmer named Tom Elwes, as a fundraising event for the local church. It became so popular that it survived till this day.

The race course is a white table cloth with two concentric circles drawn on it. The inside circle is the starting point, and the competitors are placed on the line, facing outward. The first snail to cross the outer circle wins.

The winner is rewarded with a crisp head of lettuce.

Golf's Hour of Infamy

Although most people today would agree that golf is a sport with status and prestige, it once was banned completely in Scotland.

The game originated on the east coast of Scotland, with players trying to hit a pebble over sand dunes and along a track with a bent stick. Golf became very popular among the Scots—so much so that many men neglected their military training.

In 1457, the Scottish army was getting ready for another war with England, whom they called "the auld enemy." King James II realized, however, that he didn't have enough archers to win the war because all the able-bodied men were playing golf all day long.

The Scottish parliament therefore banned the sport, and it remained taboo until 1502.

A President Playing Ball

Sometimes, it's very hard to separate sports and politics. That can lead to sports, though!

One politician who used sport as a clever way of getting into his constituents' hearts is the American ex-president Barack Obama.

In his first televised speech after taking office in 2008, Obama announced that he would make it his business to get playoffs for major college football instated. At the time, the two teams who would play in the national championship were determined by a computer, according to their points standing.

Looking at Obama's move closely, it becomes clear that he pitted himself, symbolically, against some of the American money powerhouses who were used to calling the shots in the country. He sent them a clear challenge.

While the playoffs did indeed become reality a few months later, the success of Obama's presidential career is still very much debated.

Bonus Interrogation

1. Despite which injury did Jesse Owens break three world records at the Olympic Games of 1945?
2. How long did tennis players Vicki Nelson Dunbar and Jean Hepner play for one point in their 1984 match?
3. What do Australians count competitively?
4. What is the current record for worm charming?
5. What is known as "Britain's stupidest sport?"

Answers

1. He had bad bruising of his lower back.
2. 29 minutes.
3. Sheep.
4. 567 worms.
5. Shin-kicking.

Chapter 7: Science, Nature, and Animals

Despite extensive research, humans still don't fully understand nature, the behavior of animals, and science in general.

This chapter showcases the unbelievable, and sometimes bizarre, world around us.

May the Best Dog Win

Not every man is fit to be a leader, but dogs are a different story. Residents of the tiny town of Sunol, California, had that exact thought when they elected Bosco Ramos, a black Labrador Rottweiler crossbreed, to be their honorary mayor.

Bosco was the much-loved pet of the Stillman family and everyone in the close-knit town knew him. He was frequently seen ambling around the local pub and accompanying patrons, exiting somewhat worse for wear, on a sobering stroll around town. Residents often stopped in the street to pet him.

He was nominated in 1981, as a joke, in a fun election organized by the townsfolk. Bosco ended up beating his two human opponents by a landslide victory. He had his own formal tuxedo and was often seen attending social events and pageants, dressed to kill.

He became known throughout America as the first dog mayor. His international fame was sparked by an article about him in a Chinese communist newspaper, using him to demonstrate that democratic elections don't work.

Bosco held the position until his death in 1994. A life-size statue of him was erected next to the Sunol post office in 2008.

The Pandemic Has Its Own Tune

During the Covid-19 pandemic, birdsong in San Francisco changed.

An associate professor in ecology and evolutionary biology from the University of Tennessee at Knoxville, Elizabeth Derryberry, had been studying white-crowned sparrows for several years when a hard lockdown to combat the virus hit the U.S. in the spring of 2020.

Prof. Derryberry continued observing the birds and quickly realized that the change she picked up was not only because it was easier to hear any bird in the suddenly quiet town; their actual song had changed.

The pitch of the birds' songs had dropped noticeably. The lower pitch, combined with lower volume, made it possible for the birds to warble, flourish, and trill once again. These features allow the sound to travel much further, helping the birds to defend their breeding territory better.

Ornithologists have noted that the new bird song didn't change when the noise returned to the city streets after the pandemic. Instead, young birds are now learning the age old way of singing that existed long before man took over their habitat.

The Kingdom of Snakes

There is one Brazilian island you should rather avoid if you don't want to die an agonizing death from snake venom.

Ilha da Queimada Grande is a beautiful paradise located about 90 miles off the coast of São Paulo. At first glance, it looks like all the other idyllic spots on that stretch of coast.

The hidden truth, however, is that the island is home to between 2,000 and 4,000 individuals of one of the most venomous snake species known: golden lancehead vipers. Some estimates say there's one snake for every square meter of the island.

Their venom is three to five times stronger than any of the other land based species and a bite from one of them can kill an average human in less than an hour. The venom causes the rapid necrosis of muscles, brain hemorrhaging, intestinal bleeding, and kidney failure. Even with immediate treatment, there's still a 3% chance of fatality.

Visits to the island are strictly regulated and the Brazilian government requires a doctor to accompany every group, although no tourists are allowed. Members of the navy have to make annual trips to Ilha da Queimada Grande to maintain the lighthouse, and many biologists and scientists wish to study the golden lanceheads.

Unfortunately, wildlife smugglers discovered the valuable snake species too. Their numbers have been greatly reduced in recent years by poachers who sell them on the black market for between $10,000 and $30,000. The species is currently listed as critically endangered on the Red List of the International Union for Conservation of Nature.

Tonga's Aquaman

A 57-year-old man from Tonga astonished the world by swimming for about 27 hours, after a tsunami swept him out to sea.

Lisala Folau lives on a small Tongan island called Atata, where the Hunga Tonga-Hunga Ha'apai volcano erupted in January 2022. The huge eruption caused a devastating tsunami that damaged infrastructure and knocked out the communication networks utilized by the nation of about 105,000 inhabitants. Three people also lost their lives.

Folau was caught unawares by the huge waves when the tsunami hit his island at about seven that night. Although he tried clinging to a tree after the water burst through his living room, a big wave dislodged him, and he was swept out into the open sea.

He told reporters that he concentrated on trying to float while the huge waves buffeted him. When he could start swimming, he slowly covered the 4.7 miles to the main island. It took him 27 hours to reach the shore.

His story immediately went viral, and the press started calling Folau the real Aquaman. He, however, insists that he did nothing special.

This feat is all the more incredible when you take into account that he is disabled and cannot walk properly.

Epileptic Visions

Joan of Arc, the young girl who became a formidable military leader in medieval France, is famous for receiving instructions through divine visions. She claimed to speak regularly with several saints who advised her on the best strategy to drive the English from French territory during the Hundred Years' War.

She was captured by the enemy in 1430 and put on trial. Joan stood accused of heresy for, among other things, believing the visions which her accuser, Bishop Pierre Cauchon, regarded as demonic in origin.

The English court eventually found her guilty of the crimes she was accused of and condemned her to death. On May 30, 1431, she was burned at the stake. Joan was only about nineteen years old.

Modern scientists suspected that the divine visions the brave girl claimed to hear, and sometimes see, could have had an organic origin. Dr. Guiseppe d'Orsi, an Italian neurologist, was the first to publish the hypothesis that Joan of Arc suffered from a specific form of epilepsy known as idiopathic partial epilepsy with auditory features (IPEAF).

IPEAF is a genetic condition, and it affects only one part of the brain. D'Orsi argued that, in Joan's case, the epileptic seizures affected the parts of her brain that caused auditory and visual hallucinations. That is why she firmly believed they were real and stood by her convictions till the end.

The only way to determine the validity of the theory would be to test a DNA sample. Unfortunately, no one has so far managed to come up with any DNA from Joan.

Anger Can Be a Disease

The family feud between the McCoy and Hatfield families in the U.S. is probably the most famous in the world. The two clans clashed violently in the 1880s and 1890s, prompting several police and judicial actions.

They lived on opposite sides of a stream. The origins of their bloody feud are not clear. Some sources attribute the animosity to their differences during the American Civil War, while others say it began with patriarch Ole Ran'l McCoy's belief that one of the Hatfields stole a pig from him in 1878.

The feud led to several murders on both sides, reaching a climax in 1888. The hostilities subsided in the beginning of the 20th century.

Today, scientists believe the anger and violence could have been caused by Von Hippel-Lindau disease. It is a rare condition that causes tumors on the adrenal glands. Among other stressful symptoms, sufferers have highly increased production of the "fight-or-flight" hormones. The combination of symptoms presents a textbook case of aggression and violent behavior.

The theory is supported by the fact that many of the McCoy family still, to this day, suffer from similar tumors.

The (Possibly) Moldy Origins of a Revolution

In 1789, French peasants started taking up arms amid reports of threatening brigands hiding in the dense woods. Panic quickly spread throughout France, sparking riots against what was rumored as a plot by the aristocracy to rob them of their way of life.

When troops gathered in Paris, the common people regarded it as provocation and seized the Bastille on July 14, 1789.

The period of panic became known as The Great Fear, but its origins remain obscure. Many theories have been put forward, including one by historian Mary Matossian in the late 1980s.

Matossian argued that the peasants ate wheat that was contaminated with a form of mold called ergot. Ergot contains a chemical compound used to synthesize the drug LSD. The mold is known to cause symptoms such as paranoia and hallucinations.

While historians agree that most of the crops in France were afflicted by ergot in the late 1700s, the debate about whether it really caused the peasants to act on imaginary events is ongoing.

The Deadliest Pepper on Earth

Death by chili pepper is possible. That is, if you eat some of the Dragon's Breath variety that was developed for the University of Nottingham in 2017.

According to Tom Smith, the vegetable grower who collaborated with researchers from the university, the new pepper on the block measures so high on the capsaicin scale that it can almost be classified as a weapon.

Capsaicin is the substance that causes the burning sensation we feel when we eat anything containing it. There is no real heat involved, but the capsaicin tricks our brains into believing there's a physical fire that has to be put out. The brain responds to the emergency by filling surface cells in the mouth and throat with water. The idea is that the blisters should help absorb some of the heat.

The concentration of capsaicin is measured on the Scoville scale. Dragon's Breath hits the scale at 2.48 million heat units. In comparison, a habanero pepper only measures at about 350,000 Scoville heat units.

In the case of a pepper as hot as Dragon's Breath, the capsaicin permeates the blisters and activates the nerve endings under them. This causes the immune system to go into overdrive and anaphylactic shock may follow, closing the person's airways.

In all fairness to Smith, he did not grow the potent pepper to be eaten. The folks at the university intend to use it as a form of topical anesthetic for people who cannot tolerate regular anesthetics.

Currying Favor

When an exotic-looking orange bird turned up at a British animal rescue center in 2019, the staff was baffled. It looked like a seagull, but its vibrant orange plumage was unlike any they had seen before.

Upon closer examination, they realized it was a herring gull whose feathers were covered in curry or turmeric. The powder was packed so tightly on his body that he could not fly properly. The staff promptly named him Vinny, after vindaloo curry.

Seagulls are very inquisitive birds and it's anybody's guess how he got his curry covering. Fortunately, he suffered no ill consequences from his adventure and, after he was scrubbed clean, he was set free.

An Anchovy That Would Have Eaten Your Pizza

Imagine an anchovy that's far bigger than any pizza, and aggressive too. It doesn't even remotely sound like the little salty, plankton-eating fish we've come to love in food.

Researchers recently published the results of a study done on fossils of the saber-toothed anchovy, revealing that the ancestors of the modern anchovy were formidable creatures.

They grew to about three feet in length. The fangs lining their lower jaws, with a single saber-like tooth in their upper jaws, suggested they preyed on smaller fish.

They lived 40 to 45 million years ago, evolving after the mass extinction event of all life on earth that occurred about 66 million years ago. It is unclear why they did not survive—scientists suggest they could have faced stiff competition from other predatory fish such as barracudas and mackerels.

Typos Can Cost You Dearly

Typos can be, at best, embarrassing. At worst, they can cost you $168 million.

A small item of mathematical notation that was omitted in the computer code for the launching of NASA's 1962 Mariner I space probe resulted in the destruction of the hugely expensive machine, only 293 seconds into the mission.

The piece of code, known as an overbar, looks very much like a hyphen. Without the critical "hyphen," the calculations changed, and Mariner I lost contact with its guidance system. The rocket veered catastrophically off course, prompting a safety officer to order the probe to be blown up.

The well-known science fiction writer, Arthur C. Clarke, dubbed the expensive disaster "the most expensive hyphen in history."

The Racing Line

Every one of the more than half a million thoroughbred racehorses in the world today can trace their lineage back to one common ancestor.

That is an Arabian stallion born in 1700 who was called Darley Arabian.

In those years, it was common practice to breed several English mares with only a few Arabian stallions or similar animals. Their offspring are the most valuable horses in existence, although many suffer from serious health problems due to inbreeding.

Weighing the Internet

You can take this headline literally, believe it or not. The internet has physical weight.

It has nothing to do with devices or books full of knowledge. The net consists of electrons. Although they are extremely small, electrons have physical mass that can be weighed.

According to experts, the whole of the internet network throughout the world weighed together will be about as heavy as an apricot.

Scientist Dr. John Kubiatowicz first attempted to explain this in 2011. He estimated that each bit of data in existence weighs about 0.000000000000000002 grams (7,05467372134038 8e-18 oz).

As the internet grows, its weight increases. There is no change in the number of electrons, but their energy increases and that makes them heavier.

The Longest-Running Battery on Record

Oxford University in Britain is home to a battery that has been going for more than 180 years.

A physics professor in the mid-1800s, Robert Walker, set the battery and the two small bells it rings, up in his laboratory.

The ringing bells with their battery eventually ended up in the university's Clarendon Laboratory with a note written in Walker's hand reading "Set up in 1840." It is estimated that the bells have rung more than 10 billion times by now.

Because it could be disastrous to open the battery to learn its secret, scientists have been speculating for years about the reason for its longevity. No one in the scientific community knows for sure what's going on, but everyone definitely wants to see how long the battery will keep going.

Trans-Siberian Treasure

The Trans-Siberian railroad in Russia is not only the longest in the world, but also one of the most scenic and unique.

The route stretches over 5,772 miles, starting from Moscow in the west and ending at Vladivostok in the east.

Passengers travel through eight different time zones during the journey that takes seven days to complete. The train also crosses a record 3,901 bridges.

A Blooming Stink

The scents usually associated with plants in full bloom are definitely not what you would describe as stinky. Most of them are quite pleasing.

However, a Papua New Guinean orchid, *Bulbophyllum Phalaenopsis,* upsets this picture completely with a fragrance reeking of rotting cabbages, dead rats, and rotting fish.

The plant is seldom seen flowering outside of its natural habitat, but Cambridge University Botanic Garden recently collected a specimen that flowered in 2022.

Foul-smelling plants and flowers use their stench to attract insects that would normally lay their eggs in feces and rotting material, rather than on a plant. This ensures they get pollinated, giving them a better shot at survival.

Bumble Bee Ball Game

Bumblebees play ball.

Video footage taken by research students at the Queen Mary University of London shows the bees repeatedly rolling around a little ball without any apparent survival purpose.

After observing their behavior in the wild, the students designed an experimental arena for a group of 45 bees. They placed a number of small wooden balls in the arena. The bees were then given a choice of following a clear path to food or walking through an area where they could stop to roll around some balls.

The experiment showed the bees preferred the path where they could play for a while before eating.

Fireflies in Space

When American astronaut John Glenn told NASA Mission Control in 1962 that he saw greenish-glowing fireflies around the spacecraft he was in, it immediately created a flurry of speculation about extraterrestrials.

Space exploration was in its infancy and Glenn was part of the first team of astronauts picked by NASA in 1959 to orbit Earth. It was during this journey in the *Friendship Seven* craft that Glenn made his famous observation.

He told controllers that he was watching the sun during his second trip around our planet when his craft was suddenly surrounded by the little lights.

In later scientific analysis of the footage, it emerged that the "miracle fireflies" had a far more mundane explanation. The body fluids of astronauts in the early crafts were expelled into space. The moisture instantly froze when it got outside. While Glenn was watching, the sunlight hit the little balls of ice just right to create the glowing effect.

Virtual Reality for Cows

A Turkish farmer supplied his milk cows with virtual reality headsets to make them happier and get them to produce more milk.

Izzet Kocak wanted to cheer up the cows after they were brought inside from the sunny pastures for the long, cold winter. After reading about the benefits of virtual reality to simulate a pleasant environment, he had goggles made for two of the cows as an experiment.

According to the farmer, the milk output of the two cows increased from 22 liters to 27 liters per day.

All the cows have since received their simulated sunny pastures and green grass, with Kocak reporting an overall drop in stress among the herd.

The Marathon Bird

During migration, birds fly huge distances. A young bar-tailed godwit has, however, set a new record with its flight of 8,435 miles.

The bird was tagged with a GPS chip in Alaska as a hatchling. Scientists followed its journey across the Pacific Ocean when it left southwest Alaska at five months of age.

Only 11 days later, the brave young bird touched down at Ansons Bay in northeastern Tasmania, Australia, after taking a couple of unexpected turns.

The Australian scientists are not sure yet whether the bird got lost, or if it's the normal migratory route for that species.

According to the Guinness Book of World Records, the previous record for a migrating bird was 7,580 miles. The record was set in 2020 by a godwit that flew from Alaska to New Zealand.

Bonus Interrogation

1. For how many years was the dog Bosco Ramos a mayor in California?
2. How long did Tonga's Aquaman swim in one go?
3. Which disease might have caused Joan of Arc's visions?
4. What is the deadliest variety of chili pepper on earth called?
5. True or false: Bumblebees like football.

Answers

1. 13 years.
2. 27 hours.
3. Epilepsy.
4. Dragon's Breath.
5. True.

Chapter 8: Pop Culture

Kick back and enjoy a chapter of being amazed, amused, and astonished by our fellow humans.

Truth is often stranger than fiction.

An Accidental Millionaire

LaQuedra Edwards from Los Angeles was quite annoyed when a stranger bumped into her just as she was buying a lottery ticket. She didn't usually spend much money on the lottery, but the bump caused her to push a button she didn't intend to, and she purchased a $30 ticket. By that time, the man had disappeared without so much as a word of apology.

Still fuming, Edwards got into her car and started scratching the expensive ticket. She couldn't believe her eyes when it turned out that she had won the grand prize of $10 million.

The bump might have been rude, but the prize money definitely wasn't!

A Modern-Day Jonah

In 2019, a marine photographer snorkeling off the east coast of South Africa nearly got swallowed by a whale, just like the Biblical character Jonah.

Rainer Schimpf was filming a sardine run. He told reporters that his main concern was to keep a lookout for sharks that were attracted to the activity in the water, and he did not pay much attention to the whale gorging itself on the little silver fish.

The next thing he knew, he was in complete darkness as his head and torso disappeared into the Bryde's whale's mouth. He managed to stay calm because he knew the whale's throat was too small to swallow him. It was, however, possible that the whale might dive down into deep water with him.

Fortunately for Schimpf, the whale quickly realized it wasn't a sardine in his mouth. He opened his jaws and let the human go free without so much as a bruise on his body.

Double Trouble

Trying to outsmart a judge can be a costly mistake, as twin brothers in Brazil found out.

One of the brothers fathered a little girl but disappeared from the mother and child's lives without paying any support. The mother then approached the court to get a support order.

When the defendant appeared in court, it was discovered that he had an identical twin brother. The pair remained tightlipped about who the father of the baby was, and the judge ordered DNA tests.

When even the DNA results couldn't prove paternity without doubt, the judge ordered both men to pay child support. Each one would have to pay about $60 per month. The names of both men also appear on the girl's birth certificate.

The judge severely reprimanded the brothers for depriving the little girl of her biological father.

The Triple Truth

When Bobby Shafran arrived for his first day at university, he was astounded to hear several strangers greeting him as "Eddy." When he met the mysterious Eddy Galland, the two men quickly realized they were twins. Both had been adopted shortly after birth.

News of the brothers' amazing meeting spread fast. A couple of months later, a woman who saw their picture in a local newspaper contacted them to say her son David looked remarkably similar to them.

David Kellman was also adopted, and it turned out he was the third brother of the triplets that were separated at birth.

Film-maker Tim Wardle told their story in an award-winning documentary in 2018 titled "Three Identical Strangers." It was through his relentless sleuthing during the making of the film that the full truth of their separation was revealed.

It turns out they were part of a Californian psychoanalyst's research on the nature-versus-nurture issue in cases where siblings are separated at birth and given to different adoptive parents.

How to Curve a Grade in Your Favor

Computer students at Johns Hopkins University in Baltimore, U.S. found the perfect loophole to turn their final exam in their favor.

Lecturer Professor Peter Froehlich announced to his three classes that their final grading would be curved, meaning that every student would receive a grade relative to the highest score achieved by anyone in the class.

After mulling this over among themselves, all the students decided to boycott the exam. That meant every student scored an A, because they all achieved both the highest and the lowest score.

When interviewed for the university's newsletter, Professor Froehlich said he always used the final grading as a challenge to his students, but since he started lecturing in 2005, these three classes of 2012 were the first ones to accept the challenge.

He has now changed his grading system somewhat.

Has the Tomb of Santa Claus Been Found?

Archaeologists have speculated for centuries about the whereabouts of the grave of St. Nicholas of Myra, the kind-hearted cleric who inspired the legend of Santa Claus.

One of the popular beliefs was that his body was smuggled out of the church in Myra, Turkey, in the Middle Ages by Italian merchants, who buried him in Italy during the Crusades. After all, extensive searches of the church grounds in Myra, known today as the town of Demre, turned up nothing.

Recently, an archaeological team took a closer look under one of the floors that had previously been overlooked because it is covered in intricate mosaic patterns. To their excitement, they found an undisturbed shrine.

The careful process of digging down to the tomb started in 2022. The head of the Antalyan Monument Authority who discovered the promising site, Cemil Karabayram, said he was optimistic about the team's chances of finding the body of the real St. Nicholas.

Cinderella Goes to Church

On the southwest coast of Taiwan, in an area popular with tourists, a huge, shiny, blue glass shoe dominates the skyline. The shoe is a church, created by the area's recreation section manager, to attract more women to the region.

The high-heeled shoe that looks like it was dropped by Cinderella is used mainly for weddings and pre-wedding photo shoots. Besides the covered space inside, the shoe-church also features a big open-air stage with spotlights.

The structure stands 55 feet high and is 36 feet wide. It was built with more than 320 tinted glass panels at a cost of $686,000.

According to tourist officials, a local story from the 1960s inspired the creation of the blue glass shoe. It tells of a young girl from a poor family who contracted Blackfoot disease. To save her life, both legs were amputated. That resulted in the cancellation of her wedding. She remained single and spent the rest of her life in a church.

The Biggest Chest of Drawers in the World

Do you fancy working in a chest of drawers? If you live in North Carolina, U.S. you could fulfill that dream.

In the town of High Point, the biggest chest of drawers in the world stands 40 feet tall. It was originally built in 1926 to a height of 32 feet as a tribute to the town's home furniture industry.

The remodeling to a Queen Anne style in 1996 that measures 40 feet high cost the town $100,000. The four drawers are 14 feet deep and 27 feet wide.

Two six-feet-long socks hang from the middle drawer as a nod to the hosiery industry that also flourishes in High Point.

There are offices at the back, while private individuals can use the space for meetings and functions as well.

The Bad Art Gallery

The art pieces exhibited in Boston's Museum of Bad Art are guaranteed to have you scratching your head, wondering why on earth anyone would draw this.

The gallery, which is housed permanently in the Dorchester Brewing Company, has more than 800 items that never would have made it onto the walls of a regular art gallery. Just imagine looking at a Red Sox player being devoured by a monster as he heads home from first base, while strolling through a plush gallery.

Besides the puzzling perspectives and bizarre depictions, the hilarious descriptions posted next to each piece have visitors streaming through the doors.

Memphis' Duck March

Ducks are royalty at the luxurious Peabody Hotel in Memphis. Their tradition involving five Peabody ducks started 80 years ago and is still attracting attention every day.

The story started with the general manager in the 1930s, Frank Schutt. After a weekend hunting with a buddy, Schutt and his friend returned to the hotel and enjoyed a fair amount of whiskey.

Emboldened by the fine malt, they decided to put three of their live duck decoys in the hotel's fountain. The reaction from visitors and passersby was so positive that ducks became a resident feature of the fountain.

A bellhop who worked at the Peabody at the time had experience as an animal trainer in a circus. He offered to teach the ducks to march from their pen to the fountain and back.

The position of Duckmaster and the lovely tradition have been kept alive; the ducks march every day at 11 am and 5 pm down to the fountain from their rooftop pen, to the delight of many visitors.

Lost and Found at Sea

Imagine finally reaching an island after 33 days lost at sea and finding you have relatives there, descendants from an uncle who was believed drowned 50 years earlier.

That is exactly what happened to two men from the central Pacific Republic of Kiribati in 2012. Uein Buranibwe and Temaei Tontaake set out from their home, on what they expected to be an uneventful 50 mile-trip, to get gas from a nearby island. En route, their GPS system's batteries ran down and they got lost.

After drifting for more than a month, they washed up in the Marshall Islands—about 373 miles from home.

After receiving much needed food and water, one of the men discovered that his uncle who had disappeared 50 years earlier and was presumed drowned, had ended up at the same island. He had married into the community and his children were still living there.

Egg on the New York Times' Face

The scientist who is known as the father of rockets, Robert Goddard, asserted in 1919 that a rocket can function in a vacuum, therefore it should be possible to reach the moon.

In their editorial of January 1920, the New York Times published a scathing ridicule of Goddard's ideas. They concluded that he lacked even the basic scientific knowledge that is taught in schools.

This did not deter Goddard from his experiments, and he is credited with building the first liquid-fueled rocket.

On the 40th anniversary of the Apollo 11 moon landing, the New York Times published a correction to the 1920 opinion piece and apologized. It was, unfortunately, 24 years after the scientist's death.

Explosive Entertainment

When it comes to purchases of explosive devices, it's no surprise that the U.S. department of defense is top of the list. The second biggest buyer, however, might not be so obvious.

It is Disneyland. The happiest place on earth spends about $50 million annually on explosives.

No need to worry about the land of Donald Duck and Mickey Mouse being involved in a conspiracy of some sort, though. Besides the many parties and entertainment shows taking place in the park, Disneyland has a nightly show of fireworks.

That's a lot of exploding!

Ketchup Medicine

Ketchup started life without any tomatoes. Before 1834, it was made of fish or mushrooms only.

The American physician Dr. John Cooke Bennet saw the potential to use ketchup as medicine. He added tomatoes to the sauce and claimed that the added vitamins and antioxidants could cure a host of ailments, including indigestion, diarrhea, rheumatism, and jaundice.

Con artists quickly jumped on the medicine bandwagon and started selling fake concoctions that only contained laxatives.

The ketchup medicine empire collapsed totally in 1850.

The Man Who Bested a Bank

A Russian man named Dmitry Agarkov one day received an offer for a credit card in the mail from one of the local banks. He initially thought the terms looked good, until he read the small print.

It turned out that the actual interest rate the bank would charge would be much higher than what they claimed elsewhere in the document. Their service fees would also be quite steep.

Agarkov decided to have some fun with the bank. He scanned the document to his computer and altered the small print to suit himself. He changed the interest rate to 0%, exempted himself from all fees and charges, and added a clause to protect himself against any changes.

Thinking the bank would surely spot his joke, he submitted the contract. To his great surprise, the bank signed the agreement without saying a word and sent him his credit card.

He used the card happily for several years, until one day when he was a bit late with his payment. The bank informed him that his card was canceled and that he owed them quite a large sum in charges.

Agarkov took the bank to court and eventually won a settlement for an undisclosed amount without having to pay the bank one ruble. The judge ruled that the agreement was valid because both parties signed it.

Yard Sale Treasure

Don't we all dream of buying something cheaply at a yard sale, only to discover it is a priceless treasure?

The dream came true in 2007 for a lucky buyer in New York State. Browsing through a yard sale in the neighborhood, the buyer saw a nice little white bowl and purchased it for $3.

After displaying the bowl for several years in the living room, the owner became intrigued about the design and had it assessed by auctioneers at Sotheby's.

It turned out the bowl was more than 1,000 years old. It came from the Chinese Northern Song Dynasty and is known as a "Ding" bowl. Sotheby's described it as an exceptionally beautiful specimen from that time.

The subsequent sale on auction fetched $2.2 million for the rare treasure.

Not That Way...

Even experts can get art wrong. An important art work by the Dutch abstract artist Piet Mondrian has been hanging upside down for the last 75 years.

The piece called "New York City 1" was created in 1941. After being on display in the Museum of Modern Art in New York from 1945 to 1980, it was moved to the Kunstsammlung Nordrhein-Westfalen art gallery in Düsseldorf, Germany.

In 2022, the curator of the German gallery, Susanne Meyer-Buser, revealed the secret at an anniversary exhibition held for Mondrian's work. She told a stunned audience about coming across a photo taken a few days after the artist's death, showing the art work on Mondrian's easel—facing the other way round.

The gallery will not, however, change the orientation of the piece, due to fears that the colorful adhesive strips that form part of the design might come loose.

The Highest Fall Ever Survived Without a Parachute

Serbian flight attendant Vesna Vulović boarded a plane of the former Yugoslavian airline JAT on January 26, 1972, for work. She wasn't scheduled to fly that day, but there was a confusion with names, and she ended up taking the shift.

While they were in the air, a bomb went off and the wreckage plummeted to the ground from 33,330 feet.

She was the only person out of the 28 who were on board who survived the explosion and the fall. She suffered severe injuries and several broken bones and remained in a coma for days.

After being hospitalized for months, she made an almost full recovery and only retained a slight limp.

Some Boating Know-How Required

A humorous, but true, story from California tells of two men who went to Lake Isabella east of Bakersfield to try out their beautiful new boat for the first time.

They were new to boating but tried to do everything by the book. Despite their best efforts, though, they couldn't get the 22 foot-long vessel to maneuver properly. Every movement was sluggish, no matter how much power they applied.

After an hour of frustration, they gave up and limped to the nearest marina. A boating expert looked their boat over from all sides but couldn't see anything wrong. All the components seemed to be in perfect working order.

Eventually, one guy checked the underside of the boat. He came up choking on water because he was laughing so hard.

The trailer was still firmly attached under the boat.

Dying to Get a TV Role

A restauranteur from Kentucky in the U.S. badly wanted to get a role in a crime TV series. Not just any role, though—he wanted to play a dead body.

Josh Nalley started posting daily videos of himself, posing as a dead person on TikTok, hoping to get noticed.

After 321 days of playing dead on the internet, the CSI crime show at last offered him a chance to play his dream role in the 2023 series of "CSI: Vegas."

Asked why he had this peculiar acting ambition, Nalley told reporters that he did not like talking on camera and had no acting experience. He only knew how to play dead and had perfected it through his days of practice.

Although he has no intention of giving up his restaurant just yet, Nalley apparently has received several other offers to play dead on TV as well.

The Business Tycoon Who Beat Dyslexia

If you are not Swedish, you might have wondered at some point why all the products sold by IKEA seem to have such strange names. Furniture and accessories are not identified by their functions at all, and it can feel quite bewildering.

There is a method behind this madness, as has been explained by the TikTok "fact creator" Douggie Sharpe.

IKEA was founded in 1943 by Ingvar Kamprad when he was only 17 years old. He made a huge success of his business, supplying a relatively cheap and easy way for consumers to kit out their homes. He remained active in the company until his retirement in 2013.

Kamprad was, however, dyslexic. He struggled to identify stock items in his warehouse if they were classified in the usual ways.

To solve his problem, he started naming his products after different countries and landmarks. Carpets, for instance, are named after places in Denmark. Bathroom fittings bear the names of rivers and lakes in Sweden. Dining equipment of all sorts is known by the names of places in Finland.

Kamprad died in 2018 aged 91, but his heirs carry on the legacy of the man who overcame his dyslexia.

Sea Legs Forever!

People not accustomed to being on a ship, sometimes find it difficult in the beginning to walk straight while compensating for the ship's motion. This is known as "finding your sea legs."

Mario Salcedo from New York has been on cruise ships for so long that he now struggles to walk straight on the rare occasions he is back on land.

Salcedo retired from a high-end financial job at 47 and started a life of cruising. He is now, 20 years later, still happily moving from one cruise ship to the next, stepping off the ship for only about 15 days per year.

The man known in the cruise community as Super Mario has already spent more than 9,000 nights at sea. He regards himself as the happiest man alive. Cruising permanently means no cooking, cleaning, or taking out the garbage—escaping reality in a most enjoyable way.

He budgets about $70,000 per year to fund his laidback lifestyle. He chooses basic cabins only and makes some extra money on the side by managing investment portfolios for passengers.

Franken-Tarian

Did you know that writer Mary Shelley's beloved 1818 monster, Frankenstein, was a vegetarian?

Shelley's husband, writer Percy Bysshe Shelley, was a passionate early champion of the vegetarian diet and she shared the vegetarian lifestyle.

Several literary critics have commented over the years on the fact that the monster's vegetarianism is the only aspect of the much-studied story that almost never gets put under the spotlight.

In the story, Frankenstein is rejected by humanity because of his moral codes regarding animals.

Makes one wonder if he really was such a monster, after all?

Spider-Man and the Pop Star

If the King of Pop, Michael Jackson, had his way, he would have played the first Spider-Man in the 2002 movie instead of Toby Maguire.

Jackson was an ardent comics-lover and made no secret of his ambition to play the part. He went so far as to start negotiations in the late 1990s to buy Marvel Studios, to ensure he got the role.

Despite having the support of the high-profile Marvel creator, Stan Lee, Jackson's bid to buy the company failed and Maguire went on to propel the first live-action "Spider-Man" movie to box office records.

The world might have known Spider-Man as a very different character if Jackson's dream had come true.

Bonus Interrogation

1. Why were two identical brothers ordered by the court to both pay maintenance for the same baby?

2. How high is Taiwan's blue glass church built in the shape of a shoe?

3. Where is the biggest chest of drawers in the world?

4. True or false: Two shipwrecked fishermen in the Pacific found they had relatives on the island where they washed up.

5. What was the interest rate Dmitry Agarkov filled in on his bank credit card agreement, without the bank noticing the mistake?

Answers

1. They refused to divulge who the father was, and DNA testing was not conclusive because their genes were so similar to each other.

2. 55 feet.

3. North Carolina, U.S.

4. True.

5. 0%.

Chapter 9: Fabulous Flops

Things don't always go as planned, especially when marketing a new product.

Enjoy a couple of the most spectacular product failures we know of.

Newton's Namesake

In 1992, Apple introduced the world's first personal digital assistant (PDA) called Newton. It was a revolutionary concept at the time; the first computer designed to free us completely from our dependency on desktop computers.

By today's standards for handheld devices, the Newton was rudimentary. It could take notes, manage diaries, and store contacts. Using the attached stylus, handwritten notes could also be stored.

The biggest challenge Apple's development team faced was to design components small enough for the device to fit into a user's pocket.

Overcoming their obstacles, the team started shipping devices to customers in 1993. Sales, however, remained disappointing.

In later analyses, Apple conceded that the handwriting recognition feature that was supposed to be the killer feature, only killed the product altogether. They had it barely working when they started filling orders, so the number of problems that cropped up during use was just too overwhelming.

Test, test, test...

An Alien Game

No rundown of product derailments would be complete without mentioning Atari's E.T.-video game.

In 1982, the world fell in love with a little alien called E.T. the Extra-Terrestrial. He was the main character in Steven Spielberg's successful movie of the same name.

Because of the film's great success, gaming company Atari released a video game version of E.T. in the same year.

They were in a hurry to get the game on the shelves while the movie was still current, so they shortened development time to only five weeks. Good video games typically take months and even sometimes years to get ready.

Sales of the game failed miserably. It was notoriously difficult to play, with users complaining that it was confusing and disorienting.

Only 1.5 million of the 5 million copies of the game made were ever sold. After running into more financial trouble and going bust, Atari later buried the remaining copies in a landfill in New Mexico.

Less Info, Bigger Trouble

It's all good and well to design a product to make customers' lives healthier, but if you don't tell them about it, they just won't buy it.

Fast food company Burger King walked into that trap with their "Satisfries" in 2013.

"Satisfries" were added to the menu as a healthy alternative to French fries. It was made from a batter that was less porous than potatoes, so less oil was absorbed during frying.

They launched their health product at a slightly higher price than traditional French fries, but without explaining why.

The new fries had to be discontinued less than a year after they were first introduced, to avoid great losses to the company.

Misjudging the Audience

One of the most expensive, failed TV shows is Fox's "Terra Nova." The plot was a time-traveling adventure of a family in the 22nd century, who fled a dysfunctional society and ended up in prehistoric times.

The pilot episode alone cost between $16 and $20 million to produce. Filming also went through a few disasters, including a flood in Australia that nearly cost a crew member's life.

The first season of 13 episodes aired in 2011. Viewer ratings were, however, so disappointing that the second season was never shown.

It is estimated that the failed show cost Fox about $50 million—and that is without counting the marketing costs.

A Clean Disaster

The 1970s saw the birth of the cosmetic trend of adding natural ingredients to personal products. Herbs, lemon, and honey became familiar additions in beauty and hygiene merchandise.

The American personal care product company Clairol, decided in 1979 that a yogurt-based shampoo was just what the market needed. It was specifically targeted to consumers with oily hair.

Unfortunately for Clairol, they did not think the project through properly. Yogurt is a dairy product, and it spoils. The smell of sour dairy for hair has never really caught on.

Secondly, many consumers got confused about what they actually bought. The company received numerous complaints from people who ate the shampoo, thinking it was yogurt, and became seriously ill.

Thirdly, Clairol's marketing team failed spectacularly to provide any advertising for the new product. Consumers were not informed of any benefits the shampoo might have, so the labels on the bottles were, in effect, misleading.

When Coke Took the Wrong Direction

In 1967, soft drink company Coca-Cola was put on a boycott list in the Arab world because it made use of a franchise bottling company located in Israel. In the late 1980s, Coke started an intensive campaign to regain entry into the Arab market.

An American salesman posted to Saudi Arabia, who did not speak Arabic, chose to go the visual route to advertise the product. He created three posters to illustrate the soft drink's refreshing effect. In the first poster, a man is lying on his back in the desert, clearly dehydrated. In the second poster, he drinks Coca-Cola. The third poster shows him happily jogging over the sand.

The only problem with the salesman's brilliant idea was that Saudis read from right to left. He managed to convey the exact opposite message.

His overseas posting was severely short-lived.

Stick to What You Know

When toothpaste company Colgate ventured into the food market, they realized the truth of this adage.

In the 1960s, they started producing frozen meals called "Colgate Kitchen Entrees." Assuming that their success in oral hygiene would carry them, they confidently launched a range of frozen dinners. Their marketing angle was that you could eat a Colgate dinner and then brush your teeth with Colgate toothpaste.

It simply did not fly. Besides the fact that the American frozen food market was already saturated, consumers could not associate a toothpaste brand with food.

The products were withdrawn in the same year.

A Hair-Raising Mistake

Hair care company Clairol launched their curling iron called the "Mist stick" in Germany in 2006. Curling irons were at the height of their popularity, and they expected good sales from the German ladies.

The word "mist" is, unfortunately, also a German slang term for "manure."

Manure sticks didn't go down well with the fair-haired beauties.

Harley Davidson's Misjudgment

In 1996, the iconic motorbike brand expanded their line of products with the addition of aftershaves, colognes, and perfumes. Calling the series "Hot Road," all the items had faint smells of wood and tobacco.

To their great surprise the line failed dismally. Consumers did not really want to smell of wood and tobacco, while female bikers objected to the branding of the perfume as a "masculine" smell.

The company failed to make any significant sales and withdrew the new items completely after a few months.

Tripped by Timing

Sometimes, a product is a good idea, the timing for the launch is just wrong. Accommodation company Airbnb got tripped by that error in 2017.

Their new ad campaign, launched on August 28, 2017, was themed "floating world." It showed houses adorned with a water-theme, serenely floating on a calm body of water. Some of the copy mentioned phrases such as, staying above water, and living an aquatic life with a floating home.

The problem? Category four hurricane Harvey had made its devastating landfall in Texas and Louisiana on August 25. More than 100 people lost their lives in the torrential rain, flash floods, storm surges, and winds of up to 130 mph.

Body Type Blunder

Beauty company Dove, a Unilever brand, is known for ads that celebrate women and emphasize everyone's uniqueness.

That made their product failure of 2017 all the more epic. They launched a limited edition of six different packaging varieties, designed to depict different body types and sizes. The idea behind the packaging was to convey a positive message about every type of shape a woman could have.

Consumers, however, received the message radically different. Taking a bottle off the shelf in a shop meant identifying with a certain body type—something many women couldn't do, or simply did not want to do in public.

The packaging was withdrawn after the company received a huge backlash from irate female consumers.

Finger Trouble for KFC

Fried chicken fast food company KFC's slogan of "finger-lickin' good" is known almost the world over.

However, when they decided to expand into the Hong Kong market in 1987, they hit a snag with the translation of their slogan.

To the Chinese, it said, "Eat your fingers off."

The company had to act quickly to save the franchise from having to close down, because most Hong Kong consumers opted for fries only.

When American Airlines Said More Than They Intended

When American Airlines began promoting business class seats to the Mexican market, they decided to focus on the luxurious leather seats.

They chose "Fly in leather" as the slogan and had it translated into Spanish. To the Mexicans, the slogan read "Vuelo en cuero."

What no one told the airline marketing team, however, was that "en cuero" was also a Spanish slang term for being in the nude.

It turned out Mexican business travelers did not have a great appetite for flying naked.

Confused in Translation

Another cringe-worthy blunder in Mexico happened with the pen company Parker. They used the reliability of Parker pens not to leak in a user's pocket as their marketing angle.

Their English slogan "It won't leak in your pocket and embarrass you" should have been translated into Spanish to read "No se filtrará en tu bolsillo y te avergonzará." Instead, the translators confused the English word "embarrass" with the Spanish verb "embarazar."

The resulting ad told Mexican consumers that a Parker pen "won't leak in your pocket and impregnate you."

Gerber's Ga-Ga Idea

Baby food maker Gerber is one of the best-known brands, trusted by parents for years.

Instead of thinking their new product through properly, they launched a line of adult food in 1974.

The idea behind the product was good. They wanted to provide convenient single servings of vegetables, fruits, and desserts for busy adults.

Where the plan failed, was in the packaging. They offered the adult food in the same small glass bottles the baby food is sold in.

Not many adults felt comfortable eating their "creamy beef" from a jar that looked like they were eating baby food.

To add insult to injury, the name the company chose for their adult line was "Gerber's Singles." Talk about an exciting life as a single person, sitting at home and eating from a small jar...

Bonus Interrogation

1. Why did “Satisfries” flop?
2. How much money was lost with the failed TV show “Terra Nova?”
3. Which ingredient proved disastrous for Clairol’s new 1979 shampoo?
4. Which market did Colgate try to enter, without success?
5. Why did Airbnb’s 2017 “floating world” ad campaign fail?

Answers

1. Burger King forgot to inform customers about the health benefits "Satisfries" were supposed to have.
2. About $50 million, without the marketing costs.
3. Yogurt.
4. Frozen meals.
5. Their timing coincided with the floods caused by hurricane Harvey.

CONCLUSION

We've reached the end of an epic journey through the utterly astonishing and unbelievable world we live in, spiced up by some antics by our fellow men (and women).

If you liked reading this book, I'd appreciate it if you could give it a rating and review. Include some of your own trivia or your favorite story; I'd love to hear your tales.

Keep a lookout for future books from me. They'll be just as interesting and mind-boggling as this one.

Until next time!

Afterword

Thank you for reading EPIC TRUE TALES AND CRAZY STORIES. If you have enjoyed what you've learned in this book, I hope you'll consider taking a moment to write a review on the retail platform in which you have purchased.

Book reviews are an important part of the process, especially for small publishers. When you write a positive review of a book you've enjoyed, it encourages others to choose to read that book too. It also makes the author feel really good!

QUICK LINKS

Thank you for supporting this small publisher!

Contact the author at support@owenjanssen.com, or visit his website at https://owenjanssen.com/

Amazon Quick Review Links

U.S: https://bit.ly/EPICTRUETALES_US

Cananda: https://bit.ly/EPICTRUETALES_CA

U.K: https://bit.ly/EPICTRUETALES_UK

Australia: https://bit.ly/EPICTRUETALES_AU

DON'T FORGET YOUR GIFT!

As a thank you gift to my readers, I have a little surprise I hope you will enjoy...

A FREE Copy of one of our newest and most exciting books! *"WORLD WONDERS: A Captivating Compilation Of Random Trivia, Fascinating Facts, And Curious Tidbits To Catch The Quick-Witted Off Guard"*

YOUR FREE BOOK – Upcoming Code!

"WORLD WONDERS: A Captivating Compilation Of Random Trivia, Fascinating Facts, And Curious Tidbits To Catch The Quick-Witted Off Guard"

WORLD WONDERS

To obtain your **FREE** copy of ***WORLD WONDERS***
- Scan The Code Below, Or Simply Head to:

https://bit.ly/WORLDWONDERSFREE

Read our Newest Books at No Cost Before They Hit the Shelves

Are you an avid reader who loves being the first to discover the latest bestsellers? Joining Advanced Reader Copy (ARC) teams gives you the exclusive opportunity to read books before they hit the shelves! Not only do you get to enjoy the excitement of being among the first to read new releases, but you also have the chance to provide valuable feedback to authors and publishers, helping to shape the final version of the book. The best part is, you'll receive each and every single one for *free*. So, if you want to be at the forefront of the literary world and have a say in the next big thing, sign up to our ARC team today!

UPCOMING ARC

Scan the upcoming code for details. Or, simply head to https://owenjanssenarc.com/

ABOUT THE AUTHOR

Owen Janssen moved to the United States from Holland, where his father was a professor, when he was two years old. His family loved traveling and he has crisscrossed the whole country (and part of the world) with them.

Owen earned his teaching degree in Minnesota, but it wasn't long before he and his college sweetheart were off again, traveling the world together. The couple finally settled down and started a family. He has spent the last 20 years in teaching, also teaching his own children during that time.

Owen has a love of random trivia, technology, and educational matters in general. He also has a guilty pleasure of enjoying pop culture and the occasional karaoke night. He and his family still travel during summer vacations; from Disney World to going back to Holland, and he still can't get enough of all the sights he can find.

Contact the author at support@owenjanssen.com, or visit his website at www.owenjanssen.com

If you enjoyed this book, please kindly leave a review. It truly does help so much.

ALSO BY

More by Owen Janssen

Better Than Balderdash: The Ultimate Collection of Incredible True Stories, Intriguing Trivia, and Absurd Information You Didn't Know You Needed

https://books2read.com/u/3LNVzN

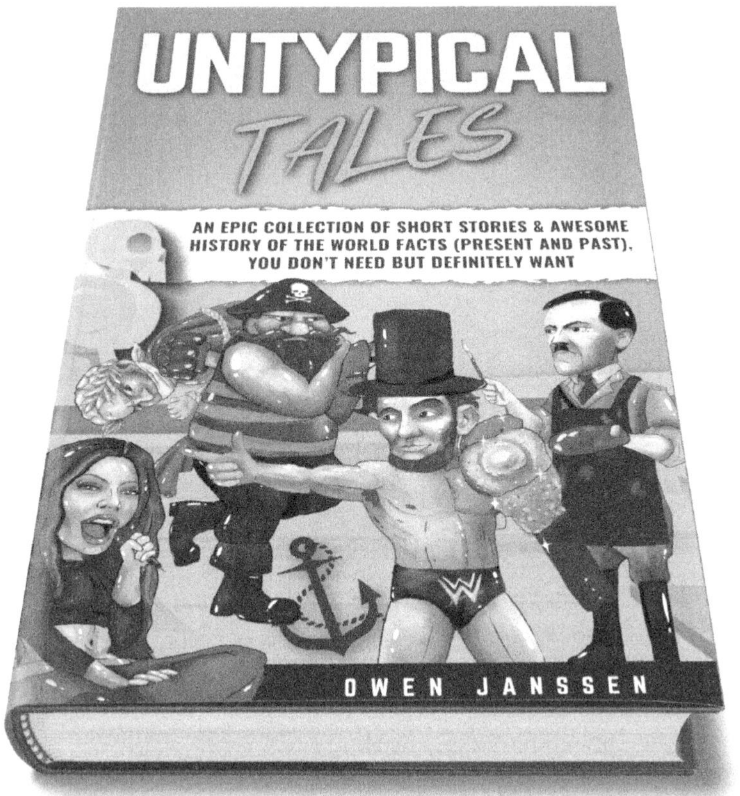

Untypical Tales: An Epic Collection of Short Stories & Awesome History of The World Facts (Present and Past), You Don't Need But Definitely Want

https://books2read.com/u/4NooaY

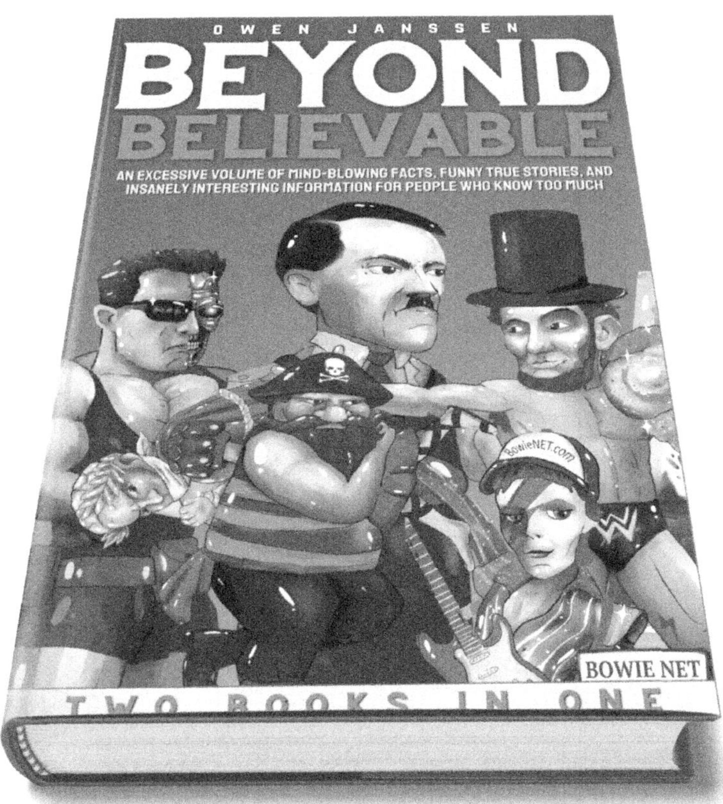

BEYOND BELIEVABLE:An Excessive Volume of Mind-blowing Facts, Funny True Stories, and Insanely Interesting Information for People Who Know Too Much: TWO BOOKS IN ONE

https://books2read.com/u/bryyWM

Thanks for Reading!

Made in the USA
Middletown, DE
11 April 2023

28616611R00096